POLITICAL ECONOMY
FOR BEGINNERS

POLITICAL ECONOMY
FOR BEGINNERS

—◆—

MILLICENT GARRET FAWCETT

1828 Press

**1828
Press**

A Baker & Taylor Business
2810 Coliseum Centre Drive
Suite 300
Charlotte, NC 28217

ISBN: 978-1-970184-17-4

Typeset by: Flipside Digital Content Company
Cover design: Samantha A. Meyer
Printed at: Baker & Taylor Publishing Services, Ashland, Ohio

Contents

Preface to the First Edition

When I was helping my husband to prepare a third edition of his *Manual of Political Economy,* it occurred to us both that a small book, explaining as briefly as possible the most important principles of the science, would be useful to beginners, and would perhaps be an assistance to those who are desirous of introducing the study of *Political Economy* into schools. It is mainly with the hope that a short and elementary book might help to make *Political Economy* a more popular study in boys' and girls' schools that the following pages have been written. In order to adapt the book especially for school use, questions have been added at the end of each chapter.

Cambridge, 1870

PREFACE TO THE SECOND EDITION

IN PREPARING A SECOND EDITION OF THIS LITTLE BOOK, I HAVE MADE NO alterations in its general character and scope. Each page has, however, been carefully revised, and at the end of each chapter I have added, after the questions, a few little puzzles, which the learner is expected to be able to solve for himself or herself; they may also, in cases where this book is used in a class, serve as a vehicle for introducing a discussion.

I am greatly indebted to Mr. E. E. Bowen of Harrow School for his kindness in suggesting this addition; and I am also especially indebted to Prof. J. E. Cairnes for many most valuable criticisms, of which in preparing this edition I have largely availed myself.

LONDON, 1872

PREFACE TO THE FOURTH EDITION

SOME OF THE PUZZLES WHICH I HAVE ADDED AT THE END OF EACH CHAPTER raise questions of no little complexity and difficulty to the beginner; and it will, no doubt, be often found that in solving these problems the student will need to go a good deal beyond the contents of the chapter to which they are appended. In order to help beginners through some of the difficulties connected with the subjects of currency and foreign trade, I have published a little book called *Tales in Political Economy*, which I hope may be useful to those young students who find that some of the puzzles carry them out of their depth.

I have only to express once more my obligations to the teaching of the late Prof. Cairnes. So far as I thought the subject lay within the scope of an elementary book, I have adopted, in this edition, the theory of cost of production, which is fully and clearly described in his *Leading Principles of Political Economy Newly Expounded.*

LONDON, 1876

PREFACE TO THE FIFTH EDITION

THE PRINCIPAL ALTERATION IN THIS EDITION OF *POLITICAL ECONOMY FOR Beginners,* is the adoption of Prof. Jevons' enumeration of the qualities which should characterize the substance selected to serve as money. I have gone through each chapter very carefully, and have altered and enlarged a great many of the illustrations, endeavoring to make them apposite to the economic conditions of the present time. I have also added an index at the end of the book, which I hope may add to its usefulness to teachers and their pupils.

LONDON, June 1880

Introduction

Political Economy is the science which investigates the nature of wealth, and the laws which govern its Production, Exchange and Distribution.

As wealth is the subject of political economy it is necessary to understand precisely what wealth is.

Wealth is anything which has an exchange value. This definition will be readily understood if the student recalls some things which, however useful and indispensable, cannot be considered wealth. Thus, the air we breathe has no exchange value; no one will exchange anything for any quantity of air, because everyone can freely and without any labor obtain as much air as he requires. In the same way the light of the sun has no exchange value. In many places water has no exchange value. Water, however, acquires an exchange value in all places where the natural supply is insufficient to meet the wants of the inhabitants. In large towns, for instance, water is supplied by means of canals and aqueducts, and in this case it has an exchange value, and may consequently be regarded as wealth.

Many most mischievous errors have been fallen into by persons who have mistaken the true nature of wealth. Formerly it was almost universally considered that "wealth" and "money" were synonymous terms. Acting on this belief, the wealth of a country was estimated by the amount of gold and silver it contained; and artificial restraints were placed upon commerce, with the view of preventing the precious metals from being sent out of the country. There are many excuses for the persons who made the mistake of confounding money and wealth. Like many others they mistook the sign for the thing signified. Wealth is always estimated in money. The income of a rich man is said to be so many thousand pounds; the national revenue and the national expenditure are said to be so many million pounds.

These and hundreds of similar facts caused the true nature of money to be misunderstood. The best way of arriving at a trustworthy conclusion respecting it is to look back into history, and see what other nations have done who have not made use of gold and silver coin. The money of the Chinese once consisted of small cubes of pressed tea; there are certain tribes of Indians who use a sort of shell as money; and Adam Smith tells us of some Arabs who used cattle for the same purpose; they fell into the same error as those who thought that wealth was the same thing as money, for they thought that no country could be wealthy that did not possess vast herds of cattle. When they first heard of France and wished to form an idea of its wealth, they asked how many cattle it contained. There have been times in the history of every country when the use of money, even of a rude description, was unknown; all exchange then had to be carried on by means of barter.

Thus if a man who had two boats were in need of a spear, he would offer a boat in exchange to anyone who would give him a spear. Though commerce could not flourish under such a system of exchange as this, yet it is idle to assert that these barbarous communities possessed no wealth, for we previously explained that wealth was anything that had an exchange value.

The real nature of Money. What then is money? It is a measure of value, and a medium of exchange. When it is said that money is a measure of value, it is virtually affirmed that any substance is money which is selected by universal consent to serve as a standard by which the value of all other commodities may be estimated. That this substance need not be gold or silver has been shown Note above; in fact any article might be selected to serve as a measure of value.

The meaning of the assertion that money is a medium of exchange is that the exchange of commodities is usually transacted through the medium of money. Thus a farmer who wished to sell barley and buy guano would not probably effect a direct exchange of these two commodities: he would sell the barley for money and with this money he would buy the guano.

The Mercantile System. The error of identifying wealth with money led to the policy briefly alluded to above, of doing everything to foster the accumulation of gold and silver. With this end in view statesmen did all they could to encourage the export trade of their own country, and to discourage importations from abroad by placing heavy duties on imported goods, and by giving bounties on exports. At the time when this policy was prevalent in England, very large duties were placed upon French wine, brandy, silks, lace, etc., with the object of preventing large quantities of these commodities being bought in England; for this, it was argued, would decrease England's wealth by causing money to be sent from England to France. The fallacies of this policy, which is known as the Mercantile System, were first exposed by Adam Smith in his great book *The Wealth of Nations,* which was published in 1776. In this work he pointed out the errors of a book, called *England's Treasure in Foreign Trade,* which was the guide of the statesmen who carried out the Mercantile System. The object of this book actually was to show that home trade was of little consequence, because it did not increase the amount of gold and silver in the country. Adam Smith's work explained, for the first time in England, the true nature of money, and showed that if all restrictive duties were discontinued the exports and imports of a country would tend to be equal.

Free trade. This part of our subject will be more fully explained in a subsequent chapter; at present it is only necessary to add that the policy of removing restrictive duties on imports and allowing commerce to take its natural course is known as the Free Trade Policy.

With these few introductory remarks we pass to the consideration of the first of the three great branches into which our subject is divided: viz. the Production of Wealth.

QUESTIONS ON THE INTRODUCTORY CHAPTER

1. What is Political Economy?
2. What is Wealth?
3. What is Money?
4. Enumerate some of the articles which have at various times been used as Money.
5. What is Barter?
6. Describe the Mercantile System.
7. Whence arose the errors of this system?
8. By whom and how were the errors of the Mercantile System first combated?
9. By what Policy has the Mercantile System been superseded?
    (*a*) Could a man be said to be wealthy, if he had not sixpence in the world?
    (*b*) Was the Spartan nation poorer because it prohibited gold?
    (*c*) Is barter quite extinct in England?

THE PRODUCTION OF WEALTH

IT WAS STATED IN THE INTRODUCTION THAT *POLITICAL ECONOMY* investigated the laws which regulate the Production, the Exchange, and the Distribution of Wealth.

The three requisites of Production. It is proposed in this section to dwell solely upon the Production of Wealth. There are three requisites of production, by the combined agency of which wealth is produced. These are Land, Labor, and Capital. In order that the various functions of these three requisites may be clearly explained, and that the peculiar office which each performs in the production of wealth may be accurately defined, this section will be divided into three chapters, under the heads of Land, Labor, and Capital.

CHAPTER ONE

ON LAND

LAND AS AN AGENT OF PRODUCTION. A FEW MOMENTS' REFLECTION WILL reveal the indispensable nature of the service which land renders to the production of wealth. There is no article of commerce, the origin of which cannot be either directly or indirectly traced to land. Look round the room in which you sit, or look at the clothes you wear, and you will notice that you can see nothing that has not been derived from the land. A piece of woolen cloth, for instance, is derived from the land. The wool of which it is made has been originally taken from the back of a sheep, which lived on the grass, turnips, etc., grown on the land. Calico can be traced even more directly to the land. The cotton plant, from the fibers of which calico is made, is the production of the land. All manufactured articles are made either of animal, vegetable, or mineral productions, all of which are derived from the land.

In fact the importance of land as an agent of production is so great that the French economists, in the time of Adam Smith, asserted that land was the sole source of wealth. It will however be shown that Labor and Capital are also indispensable to the production of wealth.

Circumstances which increase the productive power of land. There are many circumstances that increase the productive power of land. The beneficial effects of the artificial manures which chemistry has brought within the reach of the farmer are so apparent, that it is unnecessary to dwell at length upon them. Nor need we do more than allude to the modern inventions of the numerous machines, such as the reaping and thrashing machines, which do so much to increase the productive power of land, labor and capital. Many large tracts of country, such as the fens of Cambridgeshire which were once useless swamps, have been turned into rich corn land by means of drainage. It is evident that the productiveness of such land is mainly dependent on artificial causes.

Large and small farming. Much controversy has been carried on as to the relative advantages and disadvantages of large and small farming. One of the principal advantages of large farming is that it makes the use of improved machinery much more available. A farmer who rents 800 acres will find it pay him to use the steam plough and steam thrashing machine; and he will be able to avail himself of all the latest improvements in the manufacture of agricultural implements. A flock of one thousand sheep does not require twice as many shepherds as a flock of five hundred. The housing of a large number of cattle does not cost so much per head as the housing of a smaller number.

The principal advantage of small farming is that the farmer being himself a laborer, and being continually working with and among his assistants, there is no probability of the work being neglected; the strongest motives of self-interest prompting the farmer to the most strenuous exertions.

A distinction between peasant proprietors and peasant tenants. While dwelling on the influence of small farming in stimulating the industry of the farmer, it should be stated that the remarks just made apply much more powerfully in the case of peasant proprietors than in the case of peasant tenants. Nothing can be more depressing to the industry of the peasant tenant than to know that the more he exerts himself the more certain he is to have his rent raised. The peasant proprietor reaps all the fruit of his hard work himself; whereas the peasant tenant often knows that increased exertions would benefit not himself but his landlord. Ireland is often instanced as exhibiting all the disadvantages of small farming. But not only must it be remembered that in Ireland the small farmers are tenants, but that they hold their land from year to year, and they are therefore constantly liable to an increase in their rents. Small tenant farming must always be disadvantageous except in those cases in which the tenant holds a long lease of his farm; or in those cases where, as under the Irish Land Act of 1870, he has a legal claim to compensation for improvements and for arbitrary eviction. On the continent the small farms are almost invariably tilled by peasant proprietors, and the most advantageous results ensue. This probably accounts for the fact that while many English economists approve of large farms, nearly all continental economists are of the opinion that small farming is more productive of wealth.

There are some agricultural products which are never successfully cultivated in those countries where small farming is unknown. Among these are the vine and the olive. The cultivation of these requires such watchful and constant care that they are peculiarly adapted to those countries where small farming prevails. A similar remark applies to dairy farming and the rearing of fowls. An illustration of the difference between the agriculture of France and England may be given by the fact that England buys £2,000,000 of eggs from France every year. This may be in part due to the soil and climate of France being more favorable to poultry farming than those of England; but it must be in very great degree due to this: the large number of peasant farmers in France think no trouble too great if it results in pecuniary profit: whereas the English farmers are in the first place much fewer in number; and in the second place, belonging to a wealthier class, they will not give the personal trouble and attention which poultry farming necessitates. Who has not heard in the country the continual complaints of the difficulty of getting good milk and butter? People say "the farmers' wives are such fine ladies now, that they are too grand to do what their mothers and grandmothers did before them, that is, get up at five o'clock and do the dairy work themselves." This remark points out the difference between large and small farming; the fact being that in modern times the size of farms has very greatly increased; the farmer and his wife are therefore removed from the social position they formerly occupied, and they will no longer work like their own laborers. When everything has been said on both sides respecting the advantages of large and small farming, the question still remains an open one. In a future chapter it will be pointed out that there is a way of combining the advantages of both systems, by giving laborers a direct pecuniary interest in the soil which they cultivate.

QUESTIONS ON CHAPTER I. *ON LAND*

1. What are the three requisites of the Production of Wealth?
2. Show that Land is an indispensable agent of Production.
3. Mention some of the most obvious means of increasing the Productiveness of the Land.
4. Enumerate some of the advantages and disadvantages of large and small farming.
5. Why should a distinction be made between peasant proprietors and peasant tenants?
   (*a*) If the Irish Land Act has the effect of consolidating the small farms into a smaller number of much larger farms, would this probably cause any change in the production of butter in Ireland?
   (*b*) Milton exchanged the copyright of *Paradise Lost* for £15. It had an exchange value and was consequently wealth. What had Land and Capital to do with the production of this wealth?[1]

CHAPTER TWO

ON LABOR

LABOR A REQUISITE OF PRODUCTION. IN THE INTRODUCTION, WHEN THE nature of wealth was explained, an example was given of a commodity which in some circumstances cannot be regarded as wealth, and yet in other circumstances certainly constitutes wealth. It was shown that water has no exchange value so long as it is supplied spontaneously in sufficient quantities by the bounty of nature, because no one will buy what he can obtain gratuitously and without labor; but water immediately becomes wealth when the labor of man is required to convey it to the spot where it is needed. In the same manner, all commodities which have an exchange value have been made available for consumption by many different kinds of labor. It is in fact almost impossible to enumerate all the different kinds of labor which have been required to produce such an apparently simple thing as bread. Bread, it is true, may be said to be the result of the labor of the baker, but his work is only a very small part of the great amount of labor employed in producing bread. There is the miller who grinds the wheat, the reaper and the sower, the plowman who prepares the land, the blacksmith who makes the plow, and the miners who obtain the metal of which the plow is made; besides these there are the wagoners, bargemen, sailors and others, who convey the materials to the places where they are wanted; the manufacturers of the tools of the blacksmith, and so on in never-ending succession.

Definition of the exact service which Labor renders to Production. The exact service which Labor renders to the Production of Wealth is defined by Mr. Mill to be "putting things into fit places," or "moving one thing from or to another." This simple definition is so comprehensive as to include all the varied operations of industry. "Labor then, in the physical world, is always and solely employed in putting objects in motion; the properties of matter, the laws of nature, do the rest."

Take as an example the labor which is employed in building a house. How are bricks made? By moving a certain kind of clay from the place in which it is found; by pressing it into a mold and by bringing it in contact with fire. How are planks made? By moving an axe through a tree, and by moving a saw through the fallen trunk. It is unnecessary to enumerate further instances of the application of the principle, that "man has no other means of acting upon matter than by moving it" (*Principles of Political Economy,* pp. 32, 33).

Many examples of the extent to which skilled labor can add to the value of commodities may be taken from the various operations of watchmaking. For instance, one pound weight of the microscopically small steel screws used in watches, is worth six pounds weight of pure gold, or more than £280. In an article on watchmaking by Miss Faithfull in the *Victoria Magazine,* the following description is given of the "hairspring" which every watch contains: "A hairspring weighs only $\frac{1}{15000}$ of a pound troy. In a straight line it is a foot long. With a pair of tweezers we draw one out in spiral form till it is six inches long; but it springs back into place, not bent a particle from its true coiling. It must be exquisitely tempered, for it is to spring back and forth 18,000 times an hour, perhaps for several generations. A pound of steel in the bar may cost a dollar; in hairsprings it is worth 4000 dollars."

Though no wealth can be produced without labor, yet there are some kinds of labor which may be very useful but which do not assist the production of wealth. This labor is called "unproductive." Political economists have differed widely in their definitions of unproductive labor. This has partly arisen from some economists attaching an implied reproach to the epithet "unproductive." There is however no reproach conveyed in this term, unless the production of wealth is the only worthy object of existence. Mr. Mill's definition of Productive Labor is "that which produces utilities fixed and embodied in material objects."

Labor which is indirectly productive. The question then arises, "Is the labor of a teacher unproductive?" A schoolmaster may not with his own hands produce "utilities fixed and embodied in material objects," but through his instrumentality the number of productive laborers may be vastly increased. Let us suppose, for example, that a schoolmaster educates fifty boys taken from lives of idleness and vice in the streets of London; if he trains them in habits of intelligent industry, a very great number of them will probably become productive laborers. Is the inventor of a machine an unproductive laborer when by means of his invention the productiveness of other men's labor may be increased a hundredfold? These questions must certainly be answered in the negative. A distinction must therefore be drawn between labor which is indirectly productive and that which is directly productive. In the former class we place the labor of the schoolmaster, the inventor, the policeman, etc.; in the latter we place the labor of the shipwright, the shoemaker, and all those laborers whose manual work produces utilities fixed and embodied in material objects.

Unproductive Labor. Unproductive Labor is that which neither directly nor indirectly helps to increase the material wealth of the community. The labor of an opera singer, an actor, a public reader or preacher, is unproductive. The labor of a statesman is generally unproductive, although occasionally it is indirectly productive of wealth. The abolition of the corn laws, for instance, and the adoption of a free-trade policy, have caused an enormous increase in the material wealth of this country. But it must be remembered that the work of statesmen in getting rid of protection consisted in releasing trade from the shackles which the mistaken policy of previous generations of statesmen had imposed upon it. It is very often the case that when the labor of statesmen appears to be indirectly productive in the highest degree, it gains this characteristic because it undoes the mistakes of former statesmen. It is therefore very difficult to say whether on the whole the labor of statesmen is indirectly productive of wealth, except insofar as it guarantees the security of life and property.

Sometimes the labor of productive laborers turns out to be unproductive; as for instance in the case of the labor which produced the numerous unfinished canals which were abandoned about the time when it became apparent that railroads would supersede water carriage. On the contrary the labor of an unproductive laborer sometimes becomes, as it were by an accident, productive of wealth. Through the labor of scientific chemists, discoveries have been made which have greatly facilitated many industrial processes. It will thus be seen that it is sometimes difficult to decide concerning any class of laborers whether their labor will prove productive or unproductive. Before a final decision can be given the result of their work must be known.

Adam Smith's Three Advantages of Division of Labor. There are many circumstances which greatly increase the productive power of labor. Foremost among these must be placed the Division of Labor. In many industrial processes, such as that of making a glass bowl, a great number of workmen are employed, each one of whom performs a single operation. One man blows the glass into shape; another polishes it; another makes deep flutings on it; then it is repolished by another; and after a variety of more or less delicate operations, a highly skilled workman engraves upon it some beautiful and artistic figures. The various advantages which are produced by the division of labor were enumerated, as follows, by Adam Smith. First, the dexterity of the workman is increased. Second, time is saved by the workman not passing from one employment to another. Third, suitable machinery is more likely to be invented, if the mind of the workman is concentrated on a special process.

An illustration of the first advantage. The increased dexterity of the laborer is by far the most important advantage derived from the division of labor. In some of the manufactures of such a town as Birmingham, the dexterity of the workmen produced by division of labor is quite marvelous. In the pen manufactory the sole occupation of some of the workmen is to take the pens from the machine in which they are made; this is done with such wonderful rapidity that the spectator can scarcely follow with his eye the movement of the workman's hand. This dexterity can only be acquired by the workman devoting himself to a single operation.

An illustration of the second advantage. An illustration of the advantage gained by the workman not passing from one employment to another may be taken from what everyone has seen at a railway station. When the lamps in the carriages are being taken out, one man goes on the top of the carriages, takes out a lamp, throws it down to a man who puts it into a rack for the purpose of holding lamps. In this manner thirty or forty lamps can be taken out in a very few minutes; whereas if one man performed the whole of the work, and had to ascend and descend the carriages with every two or three lamps he removed, it would probably take him more than half an hour to take out as many as with the assistance of another man he removes in five minutes.

An illustration of the third advantage of the Division of Labor. Adam Smith says that the third advantage of the division of labor is the invention of a great number of machines which facilitate and abridge labor, and enable one man to do the work of many." Though Adam Smith perhaps exaggerated the importance of this advantage, there have been some very remarkable instances of it. Thus, in the first steam engines which were constructed by Watt, a boy was employed in opening and shutting a valve. This was his only work, and he probably thought that if he could contrive some plan by which the valve opened and shut without his assistance, he could spend all his time at play; he accordingly devised a simple self-acting apparatus, which had not suggested itself to the most accomplished engineers, by means of which the valve opened and shut at the proper time without demanding any attention on the boy's part.

A fourth advantage of Division of Labor. Adam Smith failed to mention one other most important advantage derived from the division of labor. The omission was first pointed out by Mr. Babbage. This advantage is that each workman can be employed solely upon the work which he can do best. It is very wasteful to employ a man who is capable of doing work worth 10s. a day, to do some unskilled work worth only 2s. a day. The old saying, that it is no good to put a race horse to plow, may be used to suggest an illustration of the fourth advantage of division of labor. To return to our example of the glass bowl; it would manifestly be quite useless to employ an unskilled laborer to engrave a delicate pattern upon the glass; and it would be very wasteful if the skilled workman, who is perhaps paid at the rate of £3 per week, were obliged to perform operations which could be equally well done by a boy receiving 8s. or 9s. a week.

Free Trade a Division of Labor. The division of labor is a great subject, and should be carried far beyond the workshop and the manufactory. Free trade is simply an extension of the principle of the division of labor. By breaking down the artificial barriers which have been erected between nations, each country, instead of being obliged to depend entirely on home manufactures, can devote its energies to those branches of trade or agriculture to which natural circumstances or national peculiarities have especially adapted it.

Cooperation of Labor. Great as the effect of the division of labor is in increasing its productiveness, it is probable that the cooperation of labor is a still more powerful agent in augmenting the efficiency of labor. Cooperation of labor has been defined as "the combined action of numbers"; the meaning of the term may be illustrated by an example. In hauling up the anchor of a large vessel the combined labor of a great number of men is needed, and in this way the anchor is drawn up in a comparatively short time. If one man attempted to draw up the anchor by himself his labor would be thrown away.

Simple and complex Cooperation of Labor. There are two kinds of Cooperation of labor;

First, Simple Cooperation; or the cooperation which takes place when several persons help each other in the same employment; for instance, in lifting a heavy weight or in hauling up an anchor, as in the example just given.

Second, Complex Cooperation; or the cooperation which takes place when several persons help each other in different employments.

An instance of complex cooperation of labor may be found in the labor which is employed to manufacture a piece of cotton cloth. In this case many different kinds of labor, employed in different ways and in different places, combine or cooperate together. Those who sow the cotton seed, and after the pod is ripe pack it in bales for exportation; the sailors who convey it from America to England; the artisans who perform so many operations upon the raw cotton before it is converted into cloth, combine their labor in order to produce a piece of calico. Another instance of complex cooperation, or several persons helping each other in different employments, is found in the assistance which agricultural labor and manufacturing labor render each other. In other words, when "one body of men having combined their labor to produce more food than they require, another body of men are induced to combine their labor for the purpose of producing more clothes than they require, and with those surplus clothes buying the surplus food of the other body of laborers."

Mr. Wakefield's theory of Colonization. A consideration of the mutual benefits which town and country laborers derive by exchanging the surplus products of their industry forms the basis of Mr. Wakefield's theory of Colonization.

Mr. Wakefield pointed out that the plan of granting to each family of settlers in a new colony a tract of fertile land, large enough to supply all its wants, tends directly to discourage the growth of commerce and the progress of civilization. A certain amount of rude abundance is obtained, but each family being isolated and independent there is neither inducement nor opportunity for enterprise, and no motive to produce more than is required for the consumption of the household. To remedy this Mr. Wakefield proposed that, as far as possible, there should be, in every colony, a town population side by side with the agricultural population. Division of labor would thus be greatly encouraged, and production would be stimulated, for a market would be found for the sale of agricultural produce in the town; the inhabitants of which would in return be compelled to exchange some articles of manufacturing industry.

The use of Tools and Machinery. Having mentioned two causes which act very powerfully in increasing the productiveness of labor, viz. Division of Labor and Cooperation of Labor, we now pass to a third, the importance of which must be evident to all; viz. the use of tools and machinery. There is no industry which is independent of the use of tools; even the rudest agriculture could not be carried on without a spade, nor the plainest sewing without a needle; and in nearly all branches of industry the introduction of elaborate machinery is rapidly becoming general. There are two ways in which machinery increases the productiveness of labor. One in which it supersedes or takes the place of the labor of individuals, as in the case of the reaping machine, or the sewing machine; and the other in which machinery achieves that which no amount of unassisted human labor could perform; such as propelling an express train at sixty miles an hour. In the first case machinery, by enabling a few persons to do the work previously performed by a great many, sets free a large quantity of labor, which seeks employment in other directions. In the second case it opens new fields of enterprise, which tend to absorb the labor set free by the introduction of machinery into other industries.

The productive power of Labor is increased by the skill, intelligence, morality, and trustworthiness of the laborer. The three principal material agencies have now been mentioned which increase the productive power of labor. But there are other than material agencies, which must not be passed over. These are the skill, intelligence, morality, and trustworthiness of the laborer.

That the skill of the workman increases the productive power of labor is so self-evident as scarcely to need illustration. In many industries the necessary skill cannot be acquired without a long apprenticeship, and it is frequently several years before the labor of the apprentice is remunerative to his master; for from want of skill the apprentice frequently spoils the materials of his industry.

The Intelligence of the Laborer. The importance of the diffusion of intelligence among the workmen, as a means of increasing the productiveness of labor, can hardly be exaggerated. An unintelligent workman performs his task mechanically; he does what he has learned to do, and no more; he suggests no improvements. If the industry in which he is engaged becomes depressed and he consequently loses his employment, he can turn his hand to nothing else; and he and his family soon become dependent on the rates, or on private charity.

The morality of the Laborer. The morality of the laborer is also an important agent in increasing the productiveness of labor. All intemperance greatly diminishes physical strength. The habitual drunkard is usually incapable, even when he is sober, of performing any severe labor, and habits of intemperance nearly always produce premature decay and death. The morality and the intelligence of the laborer are intimately connected with each other. An unintelligent person can never enter into intellectual enjoyment, and can seldom appreciate innocent pleasures. The general diffusion of education is very important from the economical, as well as from other points of view. Education stimulates the intelligence and thus makes the laborer more efficient; it also tends to make him more temperate, because it opens to him new sources of healthy and innocent pleasure and recreation.

The value of Trustworthiness in the Laborer. The untrustworthiness of the laborer renders it necessary to employ persons whose only business is to see that the laborers do their work. If people could be trusted, the labor of overlooking and watching might be saved, and drafted off to some other employment. It must also be remembered that if laborers require to be watched they will always find opportunities of shirking their work, no matter how careful the overlooker may be. This is particularly the case in agriculture, where the nature of the various occupations, and the great distance over which the laborers are scattered, render supervision extremely difficult.

Before leaving the subject of productive and unproductive labor, it may be well again to enumerate those causes which increase the productiveness of labor. These causes are divided into two classes:

MATERIAL	*and*	MORAL	
The Division of Labor		The Skill	
The Cooperation of Labor		The Intelligence	of the
		The Morality	Laborer
The Use of Machinery and Tools		The Trustworthiness	

Having now discussed the meaning of the terms productive and unproductive labor, it will be necessary, before investigating the functions of capital, that the student should know what is meant by Productive and Unproductive Consumption.

Productive and Unproductive Consumption. The distinction between productive and unproductive labor must be borne in mind, and it will then be seen that the productive laborer is also the productive consumer, and vice versa. All the consumption of the productive laborer is not productive consumption, but only that part of it which is employed in sustaining him while he is engaged in production. All luxuries must be consumed unproductively, because the consumption of them does not assist future production. All waste is unproductive consumption; and instead, as some suppose, of being beneficial to society, is in reality injurious to it. If the mere consumption of commodities were productive of wealth, no matter whether the object for which they are consumed is useful or not, the quickest way for a nation to become rich would be to burn down houses, manufactories, and public buildings, destroy the railways and docks, and pull down the telegraph wires. There can be little doubt that such conduct would soon produce great activity in the building and engineering trades; but their gain would be at the expense of the general loss. An American paper, after the great fire at Chicago, remarked what an excellent thing that great calamity had been for the building trade. The writer did not seem to remember that all that the building trade gained and much more, had been lost by the owners of the property that had been burnt. These remarks may be concluded by a very excellent illustration in explanation of this point taken from the writings of M. F. Bastiat:

Have you ever witnessed the anger of the good shopkeeper Jacques Bonhomme, when his careless son happened to break a square of glass? If you have been present at such a scene, you will most assuredly bear witness to the fact, that every one of the spectators, were there even thirty of them, by common consent apparently, offered the unfortunate owner this invariable consolation, "It is an ill wind that blows nobody good. Everybody must live, and what would become of the glaziers if panes of glass were never broken?" Now this form of condolence contains an entire theory which it will be well to show up in this simple case. . . . Suppose it cost 6 francs to repair the damage, you say that the accident brings 6 francs to the glazier's trade—that it encourages that trade to the amount of 6 francs—I grant it. I have not a word to say against it; you reason justly. The glazier comes; performs his task; receives his 6 francs; rubs his hands; and, in his heart, blesses the careless child. All this is that which is seen. But if, on the other hand, you come to the conclusion that it is a good thing to break windows, that it causes money to circulate, and that the encouragement of industry in general will be the result of it, you will oblige me to call out, "Stop there! Your theory is confined to that which is seen; it takes no account of that which is not seen."

It is not seen that as our shopkeeper has spent 6 francs upon one thing he cannot spend them upon another. It is not seen that if he had not had a window to replace he would perhaps have replaced his old shoes, or added another book to his library. In short, he would have employed his 6 francs in some way which this accident has prevented.

Let us take a view of industry in general as affected by this circumstance. The window being broken, the glazier's trade is encouraged to the amount of 6 francs; this is that which is seen.

If the window had not been broken, the shoemaker's trade (or some other) would have been encouraged to the amount of 6 francs; this is that which is not seen.

And if that which is not seen is taken into consideration, because it is a negative fact, as well as that which is seen, because it is a positive fact, it will be understood that neither industry in general, nor the sum total of national labor, is affected, whether windows are broken or not.

Now let us consider Jacques Bonhomme himself. In the former supposition, that of the window being broken, he spends 6 francs, and has neither more nor less than he had before, the enjoyment of a window.

In the second, where we suppose the window not to have been broken, he would have spent 6 francs in shoes, and would have had at the same time the enjoyment of a pair of shoes and of a window.

Now as Jacques Bonhomme forms a part of society, we must come to the conclusion, that, taking it altogether, and making an estimate of its enjoyments and its labors, it has lost the value of the broken window.

This illustration exhibits the folly of the excuse so often made for waste and luxurious extravagance, i.e., that they are good for trade.

A knowledge of one of the first principles of political economy is sufficient to show that society is no gainer by the reckless expenditure of the spendthrift. This subject cannot, however, be further investigated without entering upon an explanation of the functions of capital. This introduces another branch of the science of political economy, and must be reserved for a future chapter.

QUESTIONS ON CHAPTER II. *ON LABOR*

1. Show that labor is indispensable to the production of wealth.
2. Enumerate some of the different kinds of labor necessary to produce such a commodity as bread.
3. Define the exact service rendered by labor to production.
4. What is productive labor?
5. Show that unproductive labor is often indirectly very productive.
6. How does division of labor increase its productiveness? Quote Adam Smith's three advantages of division of labor.

7. What fourth advantage has been pointed out by Mr. Babbage?
8. Show that Free Trade is simply division of labor.
9. What is cooperation of labor?
10. Define simple and complex cooperation.
11. What is Wakefield's theory of colonization?
12. In what ways does machinery increase the productiveness of labor?
13. What moral agencies increase the productiveness of labor?
14. What is productive and unproductive consumption?
15. Show by M. Bastiat's example that unproductive consumption does not conduce to national prosperity.
    (*a*) Is the air in a diving bell wealth, and if so why?
    (*b*) Is the labor of a boy writing Virgil for a punishment productive or unproductive?
    (*c*) What kind of cooperation of labor is there in a game of cricket, and what division of labor between the different parts of the human body?
    (*d*) What are the advantages gained by division and cooperation of labor in games?
    (*e*) What is the effect of the division of labor which now universally prevails, on the highest kind of artistic skill; as for instance, Herr Joachim's violin playing?
    (*f*) Is the cooperation of labor in a game of cricket simple or complex?
    (*g*) In a game of cricket is the cooperation of any labor required except that of the players?
    (*h*) Is smoking a productive or unproductive consumption of wealth?
    (*i*) Would it be good for trade if an earthquake shook down all the houses in London?
    (*j*) Would it be good for trade if an explosion of gunpowder blew up the Houses of Parliament?
    (*k*) State the economic result of your father's gardener knocking off one of his quarts of beer.
    (*l*) What would become of undertakers if people left off dying?

CHAPTER THREE

On Capital

IT IS ERRONEOUS TO SUPPOSE THAT CAPITAL AND MONEY ARE synonymous. Capital is sometimes spoken of as if it were synonymous with money; if this were so it would not be true that Capital was one of the three requisites of the production of wealth, for money in itself does not assist in the production of wealth. A few pages back the use and functions of money were explained, and if this explanation is borne in mind it becomes evident that money is not identical with either wealth or capital. It must not be forgotten that money is a measure of value and a medium of exchange: in other words that it is a substance which is selected by universal consent to serve as a standard by which the value of all other commodities may be estimated, and which consequently may be exchanged for all other commodities.

A Definition of Capital. Capital may be defined as that part of wealth which is saved in order to assist future production.

An example of the service which Capital renders to Production. Agricultural operations could not be carried on unless the laborers were supported by wealth which had been previously accumulated. Many months elapse between the sowing of the seed and the time when the produce of that seed is converted into a loaf of bread. It is therefore evident that the laborers cannot live upon that which their labor is assisting to produce; but they are maintained by that wealth which their labor or the labor of others has previously produced. This wealth is Capital. Formerly the service which the wealth produced by past labor rendered to future production was more apparent; because farmers, instead of paying their laborers in money, paid them by giving them so much corn, potatoes, beer, cider, etc. This was called paying "in kind." A somewhat similar method of paying laborers is also known as "truck," which has been restrained and regulated by many Acts of Parliament. It has, however, been found more convenient for the farmer to exchange his wealth for money, and to distribute that portion of it which he gives as wages to his workpeople in money also. Wages are now almost universally paid in money; this money is the representative of wealth previously accumulated, and renders the same assistance to future production as the food with which the laborer was formerly remunerated. Let it then be remembered that the wealth which is distributed as wages to productive laborers is capital, and that it renders an essential service to production by maintaining the laborer while he is engaged in assisting future production. It must always be remembered that the money, in which the wages are distributed, is not capital: but the food, clothing, etc., for which this money is exchanged, are capital. Gold and silver cannot of themselves maintain labor; they are useless unless they can be exchanged for the necessaries of life. During the hardships suffered by the French army in the retreat from Moscow, the difficulties of carriage made it necessary to abandon the treasure chest. Its contents were seized by some of the soldiers who filled their pockets and knapsacks with the gold. But they did not keep it long; it was entirely useless in alleviating their wretchedness; the weight of it, in fact, increased their distress. They soon flung it out upon the snow rather than endure the burden of carrying it. This incident illustrates the uselessness of money unless it can be exchanged for commodities which are capable in themselves of supporting life or increasing its pleasures.

The wages fund. The wealth which is expended in wages is called the wages fund. It must be remembered that the wealth expended in wages is not all employed to support productive laborers. A considerable proportion of it is distributed to those whose labor is strictly unproductive. Only that portion of the wages fund which supports productive labor, is capital. The wages fund, therefore, resolves itself into two leading divisions: First, that which supports productive labor and forms a part of the general capital of the country; and second, that which supports labor not creative of wealth, and goes in unproductive expenditure.

An example of another service which Capital renders to Production. The maintenance of the laborer is not the only service which capital renders to the production of wealth. All wealth which is set aside to assist future production is capital. Buildings, machinery, and tools which assist the production of wealth, constitute capital. Many manufactures cannot be profitably carried on without the erection of large buildings and costly machinery. Take for an example the case of the manufacture of woolen cloth. The manufacturer, besides the capital which he requires for wages, must also have a vast amount of capital in buildings, tools, and machinery. It must not be supposed that the whole wealth of the manufacturer is capital; a part of his wealth is spent in various luxuries; that part, only, of his wealth is capital "which he designs to employ in carrying on fresh production." In the words of Mr. Mill, "What capital does for production is to afford the shelter, protection, tools and materials which the work requires, and to feed and otherwise maintain the laborers during the process. These are the services which present labor requires from past, and from the produce of past, labor. Whatever things are destined for this use—destined to supply productive labor with these various pre-requisites—are capital."

A demand for commodities not a demand for labor. It was said above that the part of the wealth of the manufacturer which he spends in luxuries does not constitute capital, but that part only is capital which is employed in carrying on fresh production. But it may be said that the wealth which he gives for luxuries maintains labor. If, for instance, he spends £50 upon lace, may it not be asserted that this £50 maintains the laborers who make the lace, and that therefore it is employed as capital, exactly in the same way as if the manufacturer had employed it in his own business?

This brings us to a most important proposition respecting capital, one which it is essential that the student should thoroughly understand.

The proposition is this—A demand for commodities is not a demand for labor.

The demand for labor is determined by the amount of capital and other wealth directly devoted to the remuneration of labor: the demand for commodities simply determines in what direction labor shall be employed.

An example. The truth of these assertions can best be shown by examples. Let us suppose that a manufacturer of woolen cloth is in the habit of spending £50 annually in lace. What does it matter, say some, whether he spend this £50 in lace or whether he use it to employ more laborers in his own business? Does not the £50 spent in lace maintain the laborers who make the lace, just the same as it would maintain the laborers who make cloth, if the manufacturer used the money in extending his own business? If he ceased buying the lace, for the sake of employing more clothmakers, would there not be simply a transfer of the £50 from the lacemakers to the cloth-makers? In order to find the right answer to these questions let us imagine what would actually take place if the manufacturer ceased buying the lace, and employed the £50 in paying the wages of an additional number of clothmakers. The lace manufacturer in consequence of the diminished demand for lace would diminish the production, and would withdraw from his business an amount of capital corresponding to the diminished demand. As there is no reason to suppose that the lacemaker would, on losing some of his custom, become more extravagant, or would cease to desire to derive income from the capital which the diminished demand has caused him to withdraw from his own business, it may be assumed that he would invest this capital in some other industry. This capital is not the same as that which his former customer, the woolen cloth manufacturer, is now paying his own laborers with; it is a second capital; and in the place of £50 employed in maintaining labor, there is now £100 so employed. There is no transfer from lacemakers to clothmakers. There is fresh employment for the clothmakers and a transfer from the lacemakers to some other laborers (*Principles of Political Economy,* vol. I p. 102).

This example illustrates the fallacy of the popular notion that luxurious expenditure is good for trade. No benefit is conferred upon the wages-receiving classes by the consumption of luxuries; and if the money given for luxuries be withdrawn from such an employment as farming the laborers suffer in two ways. In the first place, as shown in the above example, the wages fund is diminished by an amount corresponding to that given for the luxuries; and in the second place the production of wealth and consequent reproduction of capital are checked.

Another example. This last point can be best explained by another example, which will further illustrate the truth of the assertion that a demand for commodities is not a demand for labor. A farmer sells his wheat for the purpose of purchasing commodities. If these commodities are consumed unproductively, an amount exactly equaling their value is abstracted from the capital of the country. If however these commodities are consumed productively, the capital of the country is increased. In other words, if with the money obtained by selling his wheat, the farmer buys velvet, this purchase in no way assists production. It may add to the pleasure and gratification of the purchaser; but when it is worn out, so much wealth has been consumed without any productive result whatever. If however the farmer uses the money for which he sells his wheat in paying his laborers, they spend it in procuring the necessaries of life; these are consumed productively, for they maintain the laborer while he is assisting to produce future wealth. In the first case the purchase of the velvet leads to no result beyond the pleasure of the purchaser; in the second case the purchase by the laborers of bread and beef leads to the reproduction of wealth.

That part of wealth which consists of luxuries cannot be consumed productively, therefore the consumption of luxuries decreases the capital of a country; for capital is that part of wealth which is set aside to assist future production. But it may be said that the capital of a country is decreased by the persons who manufacture articles of luxury, and not by those who purchase them. This remark would not be made if it were remembered that articles of luxury would not be made if there were no demand for them. A demand for commodities does not increase the amount of capital and labor, but it determines the direction in which they shall be employed.

Another illustration. As a further illustration of the principle just enunciated, let it be supposed that the owner of a valuable picture intended to sell it, in order to buy jewelry. The intended purchase, if it were carried out, would have no more effect upon the wages fund and the condition of the laborer, than would be produced if by some accident the picture were destroyed, and in consequence the purchase of jewelry prevented. If the picture were destroyed the demand for jewelry would be diminished by the amount of the value of the picture; the manufacturer of the jewelry would withdraw a corresponding amount of capital from his business; but he would, in all probability, still continue to employ it as capital, and therefore the capital of the country would be neither increased nor diminished.

Another aspect of the subject. It has been shown that the purchase of luxuries has no beneficial effect upon the wages fund and the condition of the laborer, but there is still another case to be considered. A farmer, instead of spending £200 in employing laborers to improve his land, spends the same sum in paying laborers for painting, papering, and otherwise decorating his house. In each case the £200 goes directly into the pockets of the laborers, and it may therefore perhaps be thought that each employment of the money is equally beneficial to the laborers. The *immediate* result is the same, but the ultimate result may be widely different. In the first case the wages are consumed by laborers who cause a reproduction of wealth, from which capital may be saved, and the wages fund increased. In the second case the benefit to the laborers cannot extend beyond the time when they are actually receiving the wages; for their labor causes no reproduction of wealth, and consequently it can produce no augmentation of the capital of the country.

Capital is the result of saving. Enough has been said to show that capital is the result of saving, and not of spending. The spendthrift who wastes his substance in riotous living decreases the capital of the country, and therefore the excuse often made for extravagance, that it is good for trade, is based upon false notions respecting capital. If two tons of coals are consumed in producing a pineapple in March, the wealth represented by that coal is wasted, or at any rate it produces only the very inadequate return of giving two or three people a pleasant taste in their mouths for a few minutes. If the same coal had been used to smelt iron or to make gas, it would have had a much more productive result.

All unproductive consumption decreases the national capital, or tends to prevent its increase. Almsgiving, therefore, confers no benefit on the laborer comparable with a productive expenditure of wealth, which increases the national capital, and consequently augments the wages fund.

Capital in order to fulfill its functions must be consumed. Though capital is the result of saving, it must not be supposed that hoarded wealth increases the capital of the country. Capital, in order to fulfill its functions, must be consumed. Let it be constantly borne in mind that capital is that part of wealth which is set aside to assist future production; and that the way in which it assists production, is in feeding and maintaining the laborers, and in providing the shelter, protection, tools and materials, which the work requires. If this definition is remembered, it becomes evident that all capital is consumed, partially or wholly, in performing its functions. The food which sustains the laborer is immediately consumed; the buildings, machinery, and tools which the work requires are gradually consumed. It will, however, be at once perceived that the food which sustains the laborer does not perform its functions in the same way as the buildings, machinery, and tools. This indicates a very important distinction.

Circulating Capital. A part of the capital employed in any industry, such as that which provides the food of the laborers and the fuel which is consumed in the furnaces, only can perform its function once. This is called circulating capital. The definition of circulating capital given by Mr. Mill is as follows: "Capital which fulfills the whole of its office in the production in which it is engaged, by a single use, is called circulating capital" (*Prin. Pol. E.* vol. I p. 112).

Fixed capital. Besides the capital which is consumed in giving food to the laborers, or in providing materials and fuel, there is in nearly every industry a large amount of capital in a far more permanent form, such as buildings, machinery, etc. The plow will fulfill its office, of preparing the earth for receiving the seed, a very great number of times before it is worn out. Buildings which are erected for the purpose of protecting the workmen and the materials of their labor are in a still more permanent form. This sort of capital, which exists in a durable shape, and which is not destroyed by a single use, is called fixed capital.

The whole return upon circulating capital is immediate; the return on fixed capital is extended over the period during which the capital is used. The entire value of the circulating capital together with the profits upon it are replaced by the value of the immediate product; whereas in the case of fixed capital, the value of the immediate product only covers so much as is worn out together with the profit on the whole. The farmer looks to obtain by the sale of his crops a full and immediate return for all the capital which he has used in paying his laborers, and in procuring seed. But if he purchases a steam plow he will use it a great number of times, and for many successive years, and the return upon the original expense will therefore be extended over as long a period as the plow is used.

This fact explains the reason why laborers are often temporarily injured by the conversion of circulating into fixed capital. The wages of laborers, called the wages fund, are, as before stated, circulating capital; therefore any circumstance which decreases the amount of circulating capital must cause a corresponding decrease in wages. For example, if a manufacturer withdraws circulating capital to the amount of £1000, for the purpose of buying machinery, a considerable number of men are thrown out of employment, whose competition in the labor market must cause a fall in wages.

The injury to the laborer is, however, only temporary in most instances, where circulating capital has been converted into fixed capital. The introduction of machinery vastly increases the reproductive power of labor, and it therefore causes a rapid augmentation of capital; the wages fund is in consequence ultimately increased. As an example it may be mentioned that the capital which was needed for the construction of the railways in England was probably in part withdrawn from the circulating capital of the country. The laborers consequently suffered through a temporary reduction of the wages fund. But the wealth of England has been so immensely increased by the construction of railways that the ultimate result has been to increase the wages fund and the demand for labor. Consequently, the temporary injury to the laborer has been more than compensated.

There are two motives which produce a desire to save. It has already been remarked that Capital is the result of saving. It is therefore evident that increased capital implies increased saving. The desire to save differs in intensity in different ages and countries. It is generally produced by two motives: First, a prudent foresight for the future; secondly, the desire to acquire wealth by investments. In this country both these motives act with great force; this is partly owing to the national character and the habits of the people, and partly to the security of life and property which exists here. In uncivilized communities a desire to save is scarcely ever prevalent. This arises from the inability of totally uncultivated persons to look forward to the future; with such the present is everything; the future is a blank about which they do not trouble themselves. The desire to save is also checked in some cases by the insecurity of property. In those countries where there is no settled government, and where anarchy usurps the place of law, the owner of wealth is by no means sure that he will be allowed to retain his possessions. He is the object of the envy and rapacity of his neighbors, every one of whom is perhaps looking out for an opportunity of robbing him.

Joint-Stock Companies. In a country like England the desire to save is promoted by the variety of means that exists of investing small capitals, which if separately applied would not often be productive of wealth. If a professional man, for instance, has saved £100, he has probably neither opportunity nor inclination to employ this sum in any business, but if he wishes to use it as capital he can invest it in a joint-stock company; that is, a mercantile undertaking the capital of which is provided by a large number of persons. It is therefore evident that joint-stock companies are advantageous to the country, by the facility they afford of increasing the amount of wealth which is used as capital.

This fact suggests an illustration of the important position which the security of property occupies in promoting the increase of capital. A few years ago a great many joint-stock companies failed; the shareholders consequently suffered great loss, and in some instances were ruined. This produced a great feeling of distrust and insecurity. For example, if a man by strict economy had accumulated a certain quantity of money, he was very likely to reply to anyone who advised him to invest it in a joint-stock company, "Oh no! I shall not risk it. Look what our friends A., B., and C. have lost, through investing in the Overend and Gurney Company, and the Crédit Foncier." But warnings of this sort are only too readily forgotten. The promise of high interest in the glowing terms of a prospectus is generally sufficient to attract a large amount of capital out of the pockets of investors into those of the directors and promoters of fraudulent and bankrupt companies.

A Glut of Capital. Some persons imagine that no harm is done by checking the supply of capital, for they say that if it were not for circumstances of the kind just described, and the luxurious expenditure of the rich, there would be more capital than could be employed; or, in other words there would be "a glut of capital." If the nature of capital is borne in mind it will be seen that it is quite unnecessary to fear any evil results from the increase of capital. It has been frequently stated that capital is that part of wealth which is set aside to assist future production, by providing the shelter, protection, tools, and materials which the work requires, and by feeding and otherwise maintaining the laborers during the process of production. If the supply of capital is increased, it will be engaged in some fresh employment, or else it will be absorbed in the industries already existing. In both these cases there will be a greater amount of circulating capital, and the wages fund will be augmented; unless therefore the increase in the wages fund is counterbalanced by a corresponding increase in the numbers of those among whom the wages are distributed, wages will rise, and the condition of the laboring classes will be improved.

It is therefore evident that although the benefit is too often counteracted by the absence of prudential habits on the part of the laborers, any circumstances which increase capital tend powerfully to ameliorate the condition of the poor. The most important practical conclusions may be drawn from this fact, for it shows that the capitalist, and not the spendthrift or the almsgiver, is he who renders the truest service not only to himself, but to the whole community.

The principal propositions concerning the Production of Wealth have now been stated, in the three chapters on Land, Labor, and Capital. The explanation of the functions of capital has probably presented some difficulty to the beginner. It is essential that these difficulties should be overcome; for until they are thoroughly mastered it is impossible clearly to understand the more complicated questions which will be discussed in the section on the Distribution of Wealth.

QUESTIONS ON CHAPTER III. *ON CAPITAL*

1. What is Capital?
2. Show by examples that capital is a requisite of production.
3. What is that part of capital called which provides the wages of laborers?
4. Define the various ways in which capital assists production.
5. Prove that the wealth consumed in luxuries is not capital, and does not therefore assist production or increase the wages fund.
6. Prove by examples that a demand for commodities is not a demand for labor.

7. Why is it erroneous to suppose that luxurious expenditure is good for trade? Give examples.

8. Capital is the result of saving, but does hoarded wealth add to the capital of a country?

9. What is the difference between fixed and circulating capital?

10. Of what does circulating capital principally consist?

11. In what way are laborers sometimes temporarily injured by the conversion of circulating into fixed capital?

12. What circumstances produce and foster a desire to save?

13. How does commercial morality act upon the accumulation of capital?

14. What is meant by a "glut of capital?"

15. Show that the danger of a glut of capital is imaginary.

16. Prove from the propositions enunciated in this chapter that the capitalist is the real benefactor of the wages-receiving classes, and not the spendthrift or the almsgiver.

   (*a*) Is my ink capital? If I have 500,000 gallons of it, is that a glut of capital?

   (*b*) Is a cart horse capital? And if so, is he fixed or circulating?

   (*c*) Are firearms capital?

   (*d*) If a boy consumed a shilling's worth of penny tarts every day would he cause an increased demand for labor?

   (*e*) If a man kept £5000 shut up in a box, would it be capital?

   (*f*) If he invested it in a railway, would it be capital?

   (*g*) If he invested it in a loan to a nation to enable it to carry on a war, would it be capital?

   (*h*) If there is a law which permits one class of persons to rob another class without affording the latter any redress, what effect does this law have on the accumulation of wealth?

   (*i*) Is the labor of a cook productive or unproductive?

ON THE EXCHANGE OF WEALTH— INTRODUCTORY REMARKS

EXCHANGE IMPLIES THE EXISTENCE OF PRIVATE PROPERTY. THE expression "exchange of wealth" implies the existence of property. It also implies that property is possessed not by society at large but by individuals and classes. If property were possessed by the whole community in the same way as that described in "the Acts of the Apostles" as the custom of the early Christians, there could be no such thing as exchange of wealth. "Neither said any of them that ought of the things which he possessed was his own; but they had all things in common." "Neither was there any among them that lacked: for as many as were possessors of lands or houses sold them, and brought the prices of the things that were sold, and laid them down at the apostles' feet: and distribution was made unto every man according as he had need."

Socialism. If the state of things described in these verses were general the dream of the socialist would be realized. Property would not be destroyed, but "the exchange of wealth" would be a meaningless expression, for no one could exchange that which belonged as much to everyone else as to himself. The exchange of wealth consequently implies the existence of individual property; it might therefore have appeared appropriate to discuss the laws of the distribution of wealth among certain classes and persons, previous to explaining that which is comprehended under the term "exchange of wealth." The opposite course has however been here adopted because until the meanings of the words "value" and "price" are properly understood, and until the causes which regulate the value of commodities are thoroughly grasped, it will be difficult to present in a short space a clear view of the circumstances which determine the distribution of wealth into rent, wages, and profits. It is therefore proposed in this section to explain the meaning of the terms value, price, and cost of production, and to state the causes which determine the value of three classes of commodities, viz. those whose number is absolutely limited; those which cannot be increased without increasing the cost of producing them; and those which can be increased without becoming more expensive. The nature and functions of money will also be explained.

Before closing these preliminary remarks it is perhaps desirable to revert to the subject of socialism alluded to on the previous page. The fundamental idea of socialism is that individual property ought not to exist; that all ought to labor to the extent of their capabilities, and to receive in proportion to their needs, not in proportion to work done.

The economic defects of Socialism. There are many economic objections to be urged against socialistic schemes. In the first place self-interest, one of the most powerful of all the incentives to exertion, is only partially operative; a man will not work with the same energy and zeal if the results of his labor are to be shared by the whole community of which he is a member, as he will if he is able to secure the whole fruit of his toil for himself and his family. In the second place the existing checks to improvidence and recklessness, with regard to the future, are withdrawn. All the members of a socialistic society are supposed to be actuated by the loftiest sense of duty to their fellow laborers. In the present order of things a poor man has to work hard to keep himself and his family, if he has one, from want; he knows that every additional child that he has will for some years be a constant source of expense; he therefore has the most powerful incentives to exertion and providence. But in a socialistic society such a man would know, whether he worked energetically and unceasingly or slowly and irregularly, that he and his family, however numerous it was, would be maintained; he would also know that it was quite unnecessary to make any provision in case of his own death, for his family would never be allowed to want. Ebenezer Elliott, the Corn Law Rhymer, satirized the defects of communism in the following verse:

What is a Communist? One who hath yearnings
For equal division of unequal earnings;
Idler or bungler, or both, he is willing
To fork out his penny and pocket your shilling.

A recognition of the tendency of socialism to weaken the prudential restraints on population has led to the adoption in all the American communistic societies of the most absolute control over marriage and the number of births. Two of the most prosperous of the American communities are strictly celibate; in others celibacy is honored and encouraged: and even in those societies where the opposite principle prevails the governing body limits or promotes the natural growth of population as the prosperity of the community declines or increases, with as much ease as an English Chancellor of the Exchequer increases or reduces the income tax. It would therefore seem that in avoiding the economic defect of weakening the prudential restraints on population, practical communism runs into the equally serious political defect of destroying individual liberty, and encouraging an amount and kind of government control which a free people would find quite intolerable.

Notwithstanding these radical defects in socialism the upholders of the present state of things ought not to condemn it as a monstrous and wicked absurdity. The present system does not work so well as to be absolutely incapable of improvement; and though it may not be thought desirable that an alteration of existing economic arrangements should be made in the direction of socialism, we ought to be ready to admit that some improvement is necessary in a community in which three people out of every hundred are paupers. It ought also to be remembered that some of the characteristic defects of communism are embodied in the existing state of society. The Poor Law system is practically socialistic. The system of paying workmen fixed weekly wages stimulates the motive of self-interest even less than it is stimulated in a communistic society. It is often remarked that workmen paid in this way only seem to care how little work they can do, and at the same time avoid dismissal. The remuneration of many of the servants of the state does not depend upon work done. Clergymen and even ministers of state receive the same pecuniary rewards, whether they do their work ill or well, and in some cases if they leave it undone altogether. These remarks are not made in order to uphold socialism, but to show that the proposals of the socialists should not be looked upon with hatred and derision, but should receive respectful consideration from all who desire freedom of discussion and action. If the defects of the existing system were borne in mind, and if it were also remembered that the early Christians were among the many religious societies who have practiced socialism, it may reasonably be supposed that the denunciation of socialistic doctrines would be less passionate and declamatory.

Space does not permit a description of the various modifications of socialistic doctrines which have been propounded in France by Fourier and St. Simon, and in England by Robert Owen. For a detailed and most interesting account of these schemes, and of the manner in which modifications of them have been carried into practice in the American Communistic Societies, the reader is recommended to turn to M. Reybaud's *Les Réformateurs Modernes,* to Mr. A. J. Booth's works on Saint-Simon and Robert Owen, and to Mr. Nordhoff's *Communistic Societies of the United States.* There is also a short and interesting sketch of the leading socialistic schemes of the present century in Mr. J. S. Mill's *Principles of Political Economy* (pp. 245–263, vol. I). It is important to remember that socialism, or, as it is sometimes called, communism, has no connection with the principles of the *commune* of Paris. The name that was given to the section of the French people who, in the year 1871, resisted the authority of the Versailles

Government, was derived from the demand they made for *the communal,* i.e., municipal independence of Paris. None of the leaders of that party upheld socialistic principles.

QUESTIONS ON THE INTRODUCTORY REMARKS OF

SECTION II. *ON THE EXCHANGE OF WEALTH*

1. What is Socialism?
2. What economic disadvantages are connected with Socialism?
3. Name some of the principal promoters of socialistic theories.
   (*a*) Do you think Socialism would interfere with the present division of labor? If everyone received the same reward, who would do the disagreeable work?
   (*b*) If Socialism caused diminished production and a multiplication of the consumers of wealth, would it ultimately benefit even the very poorest?

CHAPTER ONE

VALUE AND PRICE

A THOROUGH COMPREHENSION OF THE TERMS "VALUE" AND "PRICE," THEIR difference, and their relation to each other, is essential to a firm grasp of nearly all economic truths.

Definition of Value. The value of any commodity is estimated by comparing it with other commodities, or by ascertaining the quantity or other commodities for which it will exchange. Thus if a pound of tea will exchange for four pounds of beef, it may be said that the value of a pound of tea is four pounds of beef. It is therefore evident that the term "value" implies a comparison; for when it is said that the value of a pound of tea is four pounds of beef a comparison is made between beef and tea.

As value implies a comparison, it is also evident that the value of a commodity varies from either of two causes—from something having its source in the particular commodity, or from something having its source in the commodities for which it is exchanged; or, as it has elsewhere been expressed, the value of a commodity varies from either intrinsic or extrinsic causes. For instance, tea may increase in value through a diminution in the supply; this would be a variation produced by an intrinsic cause. Or it may increase in value owing to a decrease in the value of some commodity for which it is exchanged, such as cloth; this would be a variation produced by an extrinsic cause. From this conception of value as a relation existing among commodities in general, it necessarily follows that there never can be a general rise or fall in values. For the expression "a general rise in the value of commodities" implies that all commodities will exchange for more of all other commodities; and this is as absurd as saying that every tree in a garden is higher than every other tree. When there is a rise in the value of any commodity there is a corresponding fall in the value of some other commodity. Thus if it is said that the value of meat is greater now than it was twenty years ago, it is virtually affirmed that a given quantity of meat will now exchange for a larger quantity of some other commodity, such as corn. than it would twenty years ago. In this case the value of corn as compared with meat has declined. Value also implies exchange, for it is by ascertaining the number of other commodities for which any particular article will exchange, that its value is determined.

Barter as a medium of exchange. In some barbarous communities all buying and selling is carried on without the use of money, by the direct exchange of commodities. Thus if one man had more food than he wished to consume he would seek to exchange it with some other man who could give him in return some article which he required, such as a coat or a set of bows and arrows. This method of exchange, some modern examples of which could be suggested by any schoolboy, is called barter; it is necessarily very clumsy, and as long as it is the sole means of exchange in any country commerce is always extremely restricted. The inconvenience arising from barter suggested the use of money. A substance was by universal consent selected to serve as a measure of the value of all other commodities and also as a medium of exchange. By the use of this substance the necessity of barter was obviated. The man who had more oxen than he required and who wished to obtain clothing or armor in exchange for them, was no longer obliged to seek some other man who was willing to make such an exchange with him; he simply had to sell his oxen to anyone who was willing to purchase them for so much money; and with this money he could purchase the other commodities which he required from any persons who were willing to dispose of them.

A Definition of Price. The value of a commodity estimated in money is termed its price. Price, therefore, has been defined as a particular case of value; for, as previously stated, the value of a commodity is estimated by the quantity of other commodities for which it will exchange. If therefore a commodity, such as a yard of cloth, will exchange for five shillings, it may truly be said that the value of a yard of cloth is 5s.; but because money has been selected to serve as a universal measure of value and medium of exchange, it is more convenient to give another name to its exchange power. The sum of money for which a commodity will exchange is therefore called its price.

When the price of a commodity such as meat is spoken of, a comparison is made between meat and the precious metals; but when the *value* of meat is spoken of, a comparison is made between meat and all other commodities. Hence it is evident that though there cannot be a general rise or fall in values, there can be a general rise or fall in prices, because it is quite possible that various circumstances might cause all commodities to exchange for an increased or decreased amount of money. For instance, if the money circulating in any particular country were suddenly doubled, while population and trade remained stationary, there would inevitably be a general rise in prices.

From the above definitions it is proved that the value of all commodities except money would not necessarily be affected if prices were doubled or trebled. Such an event would not effect any change in the relations of various commodities to each other. If, formerly, a yard of velvet was worth 3 lbs. of tea, the relative value of these commodities would not be disturbed if the tea were 7s. instead of 3s. 6d. a lb., and the velvet 21s. a yard instead of 10s. 6d. It is therefore evident that a rise or fall of general prices does not affect the value of any commodity except money. If there is a rise in prices an increased amount of money has to be given in exchange for commodities; or, in other words, the value of money has decreased. If, on the other hand, prices fall, the same amount of money will exchange for an increased quantity of other commodities, or, in other words, the value of money has increased. These considerations, however, lead to a further explanation of the nature and functions of money, which must be deferred to the next chapter.

QUESTIONS ON CHAPTER I. *VALUE AND PRICE*

1. What is value?
2. Prove that there cannot be a general rise or fall in values.
3. What is meant by bartering commodities?
4. By what means has the necessity for barter been obviated?
5. What is Price?
6. Can there be a general rise or fall in prices?
7. If prices were suddenly doubled what would be the effect of such a change on the value of commodities?

    (*a*) Is a rise in the value of bread resulting from a bad harvest produced by an extrinsic or an intrinsic cause?

    (*b*) Is a country richer if the prices of all commodities rise?

CHAPTER TWO

ON MONEY

THE FUNCTIONS OF MONEY. IN THE LAST CHAPTER THE INCONVENIENCE OF a system of barter was described, and it was stated that the necessity of this system of exchange has been obviated in all civilized countries by the use of money. This is to say, that a substance has been selected by which to measure the value of all other substances, and also to serve as a medium of exchange. If a substance had not thus been selected as a measure of value, there would be no means of stating what the wealth of an individual was, but by repeating a catalogue of all his possessions. Thus, if it were asked what the national revenue of a country like England was, it would be almost impossible to give a reply, if it were necessary to enumerate all the articles which the nation possessed. It would also be very difficult to say how much wealth an individual possessed if there were not a measure of value. It would, for instance, be necessary, in stating the wealth of a rich nobleman, to enumerate the number and height of the trees on his estates, the amount and description of furniture in his houses, the number of horses, carriages, etc., that he possessed: it would take weeks to make an inventory of his possessions; and after all a perusal of it would afford no definite notion of his wealth.

This disadvantage is obviated by the use of money, for the wealth of individuals and nations is now measured by the standard of the precious metals, and is said to be so many thousand or so many million pounds.

The convenience of the use of money as a medium of exchange has already been dwelled upon, when the nature of barter was explained. It was then stated that a country can never reach a great commercial position until barter is superseded by the use of some more convenient method of exchange. Money has been aptly described by Professor Bonamy Price as a tool for effecting exchanges, just as a hammer is a tool for driving nails. It is possible to exchange commodities without using money either as a measure of value or a medium of exchange; but in such a case the transaction is so cumbrous and clumsy that it may be very well compared to the attempts of a carpenter to work without his tools.

It is evident that the substance selected as money must be easy to carry about. A system of barter would hardly be more prejudicial to the interests of commerce than the use of a substance as money—such as wood, or iron—which does not contain great value in small bulk. If such a substance were used as money it would be necessary, when making even small purchases, to be followed by a horse and cart carrying one's money. These considerations prove that it does not necessarily happen that the substance selected as money should be either gold or silver; these commodities have usually been chosen in civilized countries because they possess in a peculiar degree the combination of qualities desirable in any substance acting as a measure of value and as a medium of exchange.

Various Substances have been used in different Countries as Money. Though gold and silver have been generally selected as the substances best fitted to be used as money, yet some countries have used other commodities in the same capacity. The Chinese formerly used pressed cubes of tea; some African tribes use a particular sort of shells; the ancient Arabs used cattle; salt has also been used as money in Abyssinia: and hides and dressed leather in other countries. But it may perhaps be stated, that experience has proved that gold and silver more perfectly fulfill the functions of money than any other substances. For it must be remembered that the substance selected as money must serve as:

First. A general standard of value.

Second. A general medium of exchange.

The substance selected as Money should possess seven Qualities.

Prof. Jevons in his book called *Money* has enumerated seven qualities which should be possessed by the substance selected to serve as money. These are:

1. Intrinsic Value.
2. Portability.
3. Indestructibility.
4. Homogeneity.
5. Divisibility.
6. Stability of Value.
7. Cognizability.

The first quality is Intrinsic Value. The importance of the first of these qualities is easily recognized. The substance selected to serve as money should be valued for its own sake not merely in its capacity as a medium of exchange and measure of value. If money were not composed of a substance which is generally prized, it would not be universally accepted in exchange for other commodities. It may be thought that the circulation of banknotes is an exception to this rule: but the exception is apparent only. A banknote represents gold: it is a promise to pay gold on demand: and it is only when the public have perfect confidence that this promise will be kept that notes are accepted as equivalent to the sum of money which they represent. From various causes gold and silver have always been greatly valued, even in the most barbarous countries and in the most remote ages of antiquity. Their brilliancy, great durability and malleability have caused them to be much prized for purposes of decoration and ornament in all ages and among all nations. For these reasons gold and silver possess in an eminent degree the first quality (intrinsic value) which should characterize the substance selected to serve as money.

The second quality is Portability, or, as it is sometimes expressed, great value in small bulk. The fact that gold and silver fulfill this condition in various degrees, is manifest. The difficulty of procuring gold and silver, their consequent rarity, and the fact that they are universally prized, contribute to enhance their value. There are other substances, such as diamonds and other precious stones, which contain a very far greater value in a much smaller bulk; but diamonds would be a most inconvenient substitute for money; a diamond the size of a pin's head would be worth from 20s. to 30s., and the inconvenience of handling such small objects and the danger of losing them would be insuperable obstacles to using diamonds as money instead of gold and silver. It is therefore evident that though the substance selected as money should contain great value in small bulk, the difference between the bulk and the value of the substance should not go beyond a certain point. Gold would be extremely unfit to make small payments with. A piece of gold of the value of sixpence would be almost as inconvenient a substitute for a silver sixpence as a diamond would be for a sovereign. In the same manner silver could not take the place of our copper coinage. In India, where there is no gold coinage, the inconvenience of carrying sufficient silver money for current expenses is very great, and leads many people to carry a chequebook instead of a purse, and pay for everything with cheques.

The third quality is Indestructibility. This is one of the most obviously necessary of all the seven qualities. If the pupil tries to imagine the inconvenience of using some perishable and easily damaged commodity as money, he will easily appreciate the importance of money being comparatively indestructible. If, for instance, one's cash consisted of eggs or cream, an accidental fall or a thunderstorm might destroy its value and consequently its exchange power. Gold is in a special degree indestructible; although no substance is entirely so. Neither fire nor water destroy or corrode gold. The golden ornaments discovered by Dr. Schliemann which have been buried for thousands of years are as brilliant and perfect as new gold.

The fourth quality is Homogeneity. This means that the substance used as money should be of a uniform quality, otherwise it would fail to have uniformity of value. Gold and silver can be reduced by the processes of refining to exactly the same degree of fineness; so that one ounce of gold is of exactly the same value as another ounce. Precious stones would be a very inconvenient substitute as money for gold and silver, because they do not possess homogeneity. The value of a diamond depends in part on its brilliancy and color and these vary very much; so that it does not at all follow that two diamonds of equal weight and size and equally well cut have equal values.

The fifth quality is Divisibility, without loss of value. Two half ounces of gold are exactly equal in value to one ounce, but with many substances division would greatly reduce the value. With rough diamonds, for instance, the rule for finding the value is to square the number of carats and multiply by the value of one carat. Thus taking the value of one carat to be two pounds we find a diamond of 6 carats to be worth £72, and a diamond of 12 carats to be worth £288; $6 \times 6 \times 2 = 72$. $12 \times 12 \times 2 = 288$. It therefore appears that a diamond of twelve carats could not be divided into two of 6 carats each without losing half its value.

The sixth quality is Stability of Value. This uniformity of value, is of great importance with regard to the first function of money, i.e., to act as a general standard of value. It is impossible from the nature of things that there should be any absolutely invariable standard of value. It was one of the economic schemes originated by Robert Owen to make labor the standard of value, and to enact that a fixed and uniform value should always attach to an hour's labor. It is obvious, however, that the value of labor is more variable than almost anything else that could have been thought of; and that there is no reason either in justice or common sense why an hour's labor from such a man as Sir Joshua Reynolds should exchange at an equal value for an hour's labor of the man who blacked his shoes. Owen's Labor Exchange which had a short-lived popularity in the year 1832 was soon broken up through its inherent error of valuing all labor alike.

All substances known to us are liable to variations in their value. The utmost that can be obtained, therefore, in the substance selected as money is that the variations in value should be slight and gradual. If the value of the substance selected as money fluctuated very rapidly, the terms of every monetary contract would be disturbed. Suppose, for instance, wheat was selected as a general standard of value; in this case if *A.* borrowed 10,000 qrs. of wheat from *B.,* promising to pay him at the end of 6 months, when the time to pay arrived the value of wheat might have increased or decreased, owing to quite unforeseen circumstances, as much as 20 or 30 percent. If the value of wheat had increased 30 percent, *A.* would virtually have to repay to *B.* 30 percent more than he borrowed; because the same quantity of wheat would exchange for 30 percent more wealth than it would have done 6 months before. If therefore the value of the substance selected to serve as money were subject to sudden fluctuations every commercial transaction would be reduced to a gambling speculation, for no one could with certainty foretell what would be the value of money in a few months' time.

The value of gold and silver varies less than that of almost any commodities which also possess the other characteristics which qualify a substance to fulfill the functions of money.

The seventh quality is Cognizability. It should be easy to recognize if money is genuine. The sound which gold makes when rung on a counter is a ready test which is often used: the absence of smell or taste is another way of distinguishing false coin from true. In order to ensure cognizability the substance used as money should be *coinable,* and the coining of money should be performed by the Government; the whole credit of the State is then pledged to ensure that the money in circulation is of full weight and of a given fineness of metal. It will be evident on consideration that many of the seven qualities just enumerated react upon each other. For instance, the portability and the indestructibility of gold are among the principal causes of its possessing the sixth quality: stability of value. A commodity which is very bulky in proportion to its value, commands very different prices in different localities: coal, for instance, is 6s. a ton at the pit's mouth and £1. 2*s*. 0*d*. a ton in London. But if a commodity can be transferred at a trifling cost from the place where its value is lower to that in which it is higher, a tendency is constantly in operation to preserve approximate uniformity of value. So also with the quality of indestructibility. All commodities which are perishable or the annual supply of which is ordinarily consumed within the year are liable to great fluctuations of value. A perishable commodity such as fresh fish must be sold within a limited period. Customers must be had at any price and accordingly in Billingsgate market, the price of fish often varies on the same day to 50 or 100 percent. Corn is not easily destructible if it is well stored, but it is liable to great variations in value owing to the fact that the annual supply is ordinarily consumed within the year; if the corn harvest all over the world is 30 percent short of the average, the whole of the world's supply of corn for the year would be reduced by 30 percent and the rise in value of corn would be enormous. But if the annual supply of gold fell off 30 percent the effect on the value of gold would hardly be felt at all, because the diminution in the annual supply of 30 percent would only affect to a very trifling degree the entire stock of gold in the world.

The meaning of a Double Standard of Value. It is sometimes proposed that what is called a double standard of value should be adopted. The meaning of the expression "double standard" is, that it should be legal to offer either gold or silver in payment of any debt, no matter what the amount of it may be. There are obvious disadvantages in this plan. Suppose that, owing to any circumstances, the value of silver declined between the time when a debt was contracted and when it was paid; it would then be to the advantage of the person who had incurred the debt to discharge it in silver instead of gold. But, as previously shown, if the standard of value fluctuates between the incurring of a debt and the payment of it, the terms of every monetary contract are disturbed, and a most disastrous effect is produced on commerce. For example, *A*. lends *B*. £25, *B*. promising to pay at the end of a year; it is quite possible that the relative value of gold and silver may have changed before the time arrives for discharging the debt. If *B.* is allowed to choose whether he will repay the loan in gold or silver, he may avail himself of any change that has taken place in the value of either silver or gold. If gold has declined in value, he can discharge his debt in gold; if silver is less valuable, he may pay his debt in silver. Hence, if there is a double standard, the terms of every monetary contract are liable to be disturbed by the fluctuations in the value of two substances, instead of being influenced only by one, as in those cases where there is a single standard of value.

There is not a Double Standard in this Country. It may be thought that as in this country there are gold, silver, and copper coins in circulation, there is not only a double, but a treble standard. This is not, however, the case. The silver and copper coinages are subsidiary. Their representative value is greater than their intrinsic value. If the silver contained in twenty shillings were melted down, its exchange value would be less than £1 sterling. Two new half crowns weigh one ounce; but the price of silver, which is quoted almost daily in the newspapers, has for several years been lower than 60*d.* per ounce. The present price (June 1880) is 52*d.* per ounce. The English silver and copper coins are issued and used because they provide a convenient means of making small payments; but they are not legal tender beyond a certain amount. No debt of more than 40*s.* can be discharged in silver unless the creditor consents; and, in the same way, no debt of more than 1*s.* can be discharged in copper. The bronze of which pence and half-pence are made is worth about 10*d.* per pound troy, and this weight will make nearly 40 pennies. The government therefore make a profit on all the silver and bronze coins they issue. These subsidiary or token coins are really akin in their nature to banknotes, insofar as their intrinsic value is less than their nominal value. Great injustice would be done if it were attempted to make these token coins legal tender for an unlimited amount, but as it is no one is injured; the government make a profit which renders it possible to remit taxation, and the public are supplied with a much more convenient coinage than they would have if every penny contained copper of the value of ½₄₀th part of a pound sterling; for in this case every penny would weigh about 2 ounces (as much as 4 half crowns) and the inconvenience of carrying such coins would be felt by everyone. Another inconvenience would arise if it were endeavored to make every penny exactly equal in value to ½₄₀th part of a sovereign; for the weight of these pennies would have to be altered with every fluctuation in the value of copper.

An Illustration from M. Bastiat. With one more observation on the subject of money this chapter will be concluded. An immense number of fallacies have been committed under the idea that money is the sole source of wealth. Everyone has most likely observed that the more money he has the richer he is, and this observation has led to the conclusion that the more money there is in circulation the richer will be the community which possesses it. The error of this conclusion is well illustrated by the following example of M. Bastiat:

Ten men sat down to play a game, in which they agreed to stake 1000 francs. Each man was provided with 10 counters, each counter representing 10 francs. When the game was finished, each received as many times 10 francs as he happened to have counters. One of the party, who was more of an arithmetician than a logician, remarked that he always found at the end of the game that he was richer in proportion as he had a greater number of counters, and asked the others if they had observed the same thing. "What holds in my case," said he, "must hold in yours, for what is true of each must be true of all." He proposed, therefore, that each should have double the former number of counters. No sooner said than done. Double the number of counters were distributed; but when the party finally rose from play, they found themselves no richer than before. The stake had not been increased, and fell to be proportionally divided. Each man, no doubt, had double the number of counters, but each counter, instead of being worth 10 francs was found to be worth only 5; and it was at length discovered that what is true of each is not always true of all.

QUESTIONS ON CHAPTER II. *ON MONEY*

1. What are the functions of money?
2. Describe what is meant by a measure of value; and give an illustration.
3. Describe what is meant by a medium of exchange; and give an illustration.
4. Is the substance selected as money necessarily gold or silver?
5. What substances have been used at different times and in different countries as money?
6. Enumerate the qualities which the substance selected as money should possess.
7. Explain and illustrate the importance of each of these qualities.
8. What substances possess these qualities in an eminent degree?
9. What are the special disadvantages of using labor as the standard of value?
10. What is meant by a "double standard of value"?
11. What are the disadvantages of a double standard?
12. Is there a double standard in this country?
13. Repeat the excellent example by means of which M. Bastiat has illustrated the true nature of money.

    (*a*) In India there is no gold coinage. What should you say was the effect of this on the mode of paying small debts? If you had £10 to pay away in about ten different shops, should you like to start out for the purpose with 100 florins in your pocket?

    (*b*) Does a man who discovers a gold mine add to the wealth of the country?

    (*c*) What would be the effect on the general wealth if everyone suddenly found that the quantity of money in his possession was doubled?

    (*d*) Would buying and selling come to an end if all the gold, silver, and copper in the world were destroyed?

CHAPTER THREE

THE VALUE OF COMMODITIES

COMMODITIES, WHEN CONSIDERED IN RELATION TO THEIR VALUE, MAY BE divided into Three Classes.

First. Those which possess a monopoly value, and whose supply cannot be increased; such as the pictures of a deceased artist.

Second. Those whose cost of production increases as an additional supply is produced; such as agricultural and mineral produce.

Third. Those whose supply can be increased without increasing their cost of production, such as manufactured commodities.

Cost of Production. In enumerating these three classes of commodities the expression "Cost of Production" has been employed. Mr. Mill has defined "cost of production," as consisting mainly of wages and profits. Prof. Cairnes, however, has adopted a different definition, and one which seems more in harmony with the actual facts of the case: he has shown that the *ultimate* elements of cost of production are toil, abstinence and risk, the first of which is endured by the laborer, the second by the capitalist, and the third in varying proportions, by both the laborer and the capitalist. The reward of the toil and risk of the laborer is wages; the reward of the abstinence and risk of the capitalist is profits. It is evident that where the competition of labor and capital is such as to ensure that the amount of wages and profits in all trades shall be strictly proportionate to the toil, risk and abstinence endured, that profits and wages are the pecuniary measure of the real cost of production; and in such cases it is a matter of indifference whether in economic reasoning cost of production is defined as consisting of wages and profits, or of toil, abstinence and risk.

Before particularizing the causes which regulate the value of the three classes of commodities above mentioned, it will be necessary to enter into an explanation of demand and supply in their relation to value. It may, perhaps, simplify the investigation if we use the word price instead of value. There is no inaccuracy in doing this, because, as previously explained, price is a particular case of value: the supposition must, however, be made that any change in the price of a commodity is produced by some change in the value of the commodity itself, and not by any change in the value of gold. Thus, if it is said that the price of tea has risen, it must be supposed that this rise is produced by an increase in the value of tea, and not by a decrease in the value of gold.

The effect of Demand and Supply upon Prices. It is often said that the price of a commodity depends on demand and supply; this is perfectly true, but the expression is sometimes used by those who could not clearly define its signification. The real relation between prices and demand and supply may be briefly expressed thus: the price of commodities must be such as to equalize the demand with the supply. As a general rule the demand increases with a diminution of the price, and as the price increases the demand diminishes. Suppose, for instance, that a house is going to be sold by auction, and that there are six persons who wish to buy it; they will compete against each other for the purchase of the house. The price of the house will be gradually raised, until at length five out of the six competitors retire from the contest, and the house becomes the property of him who offers the highest price for it; this price must be such as to cause the other competitors to withdraw their demand. For, if this be not the case, and if the other competitors offer the same or a higher price for the house, the contest will be unconcluded. When, therefore, there is free competition between the buyers and sellers of commodities, the market price of any article must be such as to equalize the supply to the demand. In the example just given six persons, *A.*, *B.*, *C.*, *D.*, *E.*, and *F.*, desire to purchase a house; the price, therefore, of the house is raised to such a point as to oblige *B., C., D., E.,* and *F.* to withdraw their demand; the only demand which remains is that of *A.*; the demand is therefore made equal to the supply.

It is however evident that in such a case as that just described, the price which the house fetches may be such as to provide a greater reward for the capital and labor engaged in building the house, than is current in the trade. If this is so the supply of houses will be increased as quickly as the circumstances of the case permit. But this increased supply will tend to reduce the price of houses to such a point that the reward obtained by the labor and capital engaged in the trade returns to its ordinary level. In a similar way if the price which the house fetches, yields less than the ordinary reward to capital and labor, the master builders and laborers will employ their capital and labor in other industries: the supply of houses will fall off, until prices return to such a point as to pay the capitalist and laborer the current profits and wages of the trade.

This continual variation of market price, on either side of the *normal* price, or that regulated by cost of production, has been compared by Mr. Mill to the perpetual fluctuation of the waves of the sea. "The sea everywhere tends to a level, its surface is always ruffled by waves, and often agitated by storms. It is enough that no point, at least in the open sea, is permanently higher than another. Each place is alternately elevated and depressed; but the ocean preserves its level."

The circumstances which regulate the Price of the first of the three classes of Commodities. It has just been stated that when exceptionally high profits are realized by the sale of any particular commodity the supply of it is stimulated, and that an effect is thus produced which reduces profits and prices to their natural rate.

There are, however, some commodities the supply of which cannot be increased, however high a price they realize. The prices, therefore, of such articles as the pictures of the old masters, ancient sculptures, the wine of any particular vintage, rare prints and books, never permanently approximate to the original cost of producing them. What, then, it may be asked, regulates the price of such commodities? As previously explained, the price of these articles must be such as to equalize the demand with the supply. To some this may seem impossible, for it may be said that everyone would like to possess one of Raphael's pictures; the demand, therefore, is indefinitely large, while the supply is small and stationary. It now becomes necessary to define what is meant by demand; it cannot be merely the desire to possess the commodity, for nearly everyone would desire to possess a Raphael. Desire for a commodity does not constitute demand unless it is combined with the power of purchasing; this combination of a wish to possess with a power to purchase has been aptly called "effectual demand." It is this effectual demand only that exercises an influence on prices. Here, then, we see two things, demand and price, each depending on the other. The demand depends on the price, as the price increases the demand decreases; and the price depends on the demand. The supply is a fixed quantity; the equality ultimately to be produced between the demand and supply cannot be accomplished by increasing the supply, it must therefore be produced by increasing the price to such a point that all demand is withdrawn save that which is equal to the supply. Let it be supposed that a picture of a deceased artist is offered for sale. If the price were fixed at £100 perhaps thousands of people would wish to buy it; if the price were raised to £500 the demand might be reduced to fifty people; if the price were still further raised to £1000 the demand might be reduced to ten persons, who would keenly compete against each other for the possession of the picture. Finally, the price might be pushed up to £1800, and the demand might be reduced to that of two individuals, A. and B. B. has perhaps decided not to give more than £1900 for the picture, whereas A. might be willing to give as much as £2000. The price, therefore, will be fixed at some point between £1900 and £2000. What this point shall be, is determined by what Adam Smith termed the higgling of the market. The owner of the picture may know that A. will give £2000 rather than lose the picture; whereas A. may not know that B. has determined to give no more than £1900. In such a case the owner of the picture may induce A. to give him £2000 for it; but if A. knows that B. will only offer

£1900, and that the owner of the picture is determined to sell, he will of course offer a sum only slightly exceeding £1900. We may suppose this sum to be £1910. At this point the effectual demand is equal to the supply; for *B.* withdraws his demand when the price exceeds £1900, and the only demand which remains is that of *A.,* who becomes the possessor of the picture.

Every article which has an exchange value is characterized by two qualities, viz.: Value in use, and Difficulty of obtaining it.

The inquiry into the causes which regulate the price of such a commodity as a picture of a deceased artist is not yet exhausted. It may be asked, Why should *A.* be willing to give £2000 for the picture while *B.* will only offer £1900? This question leads to a further investigation of the elements of value. The exchange value of every commodity is influenced by two circumstances; its intrinsic utility or value in use, and difficulty of attainment.

Under the first head, value in use, are comprehended those qualities which satisfy some want or gratify some desire. Both these elements are present in every commodity which has an exchange value. Where difficulty of attainment is absent, an article, however indispensable or beautiful, possesses no exchange value. Thus air, though indispensable to life, ordinarily possesses no exchange value, because everyone can obtain without difficulty as much air as he requires. But the air in a diving bell has an exchange value, because it would be impossible to obtain it without an expenditure of labor and capital.

The most beautiful flowers have no exchange value in the meadows and woods where they grow, because there everyone can obtain as many of them as he pleases. But they possess exchange value when they are brought into towns, for here the element "difficulty of attainment" again becomes active.

On the other hand, where "value in use" is absent no commodity has an exchange value, however difficult it may be to obtain; for no one will purchase that which neither satisfies a want nor gratifies a desire. The top brick in the chimney would have a large supply of "difficulty of attainment," but its value in use would not be more than that of any other brick, and therefore it would not have more exchange value.

The price of commodities is influenced in different degrees by these two elements. "Difficulty of attainment" generally exerts more influence in regulating the price of an article than "value in use." For instance, the value in use of a pair of boots is so great, that probably few would dispense with them if they cost five guineas a pair. But in this case the element "value in use" is only partially operative, and the price is almost entirely determined by "difficulty of attainment." It must however be remembered that value in use is always present, otherwise the article would command no price whatever. It has been explained that "effectual demand" consists of a wish to possess combined with a power to purchase. It is this effectual demand which influences the price of commodities. It is evident that "a wish to possess" any article is absolutely controlled by its value in use, that is, its power to satisfy some want or gratify some desire. The power to purchase any article is, on the other hand, controlled by the difficulty of its attainment. Thus, if a man came to me and offered to sell me 100 hearses, a great bargain, I should not be in the least inclined to close with him, because the hearses would have "no value in use" to me, and therefore I should have "no wish to possess" them. On the other hand, if I knew that on a certain day such pictures as the Rembrandts in the National Gallery were going to be sold by auction, I should not therefore think it possible that I could become the possessor of one of them. My "desire to have" them would be very great; but "the power to purchase" would be entirely absent, because the "difficulty of attainment" of such treasures would send the price up far beyond my reach.

In the previous example of the causes which regulate the price of such a commodity as one of Raphael's pictures, the element "value in use" is more operative than "difficulty of attainment." The difficulty of attainment is the same to A. and B.; the supply is absolutely limited, the price is therefore determined by the pecuniary value which A. and B. respectively set upon the gratification they will derive from possessing the picture. It is impossible here to analyze the causes which make A. fix upon £2000 as the pecuniary value of the pleasure he will derive from the picture, while B. thinks his desire for it is not worth more than £1900. It is quite possible that each possesses an equal desire for the picture, and that it would afford them both an equal amount of gratification; but *B.* may be a less wealthy man than *A.*, and he may therefore not feel justified in spending an equally large sum in the purchase of the picture.

It is therefore evident that the price of an article, the supply of which is absolutely limited, is mainly determined by the pecuniary value which certain individuals set upon its power to satisfy some want or gratify some desire; difficulty of attainment is not however absent, even in this case; because the price diminishes as the difficulty of attainment decreases, and would cease to exist if difficulty of attainment were entirely absent.

The price of Agricultural Produce. The causes must now be examined which regulate the price of those commodities whose supply can only be increased by a greater proportional outlay of labor and capital, and which therefore become more expensive as the supply is increased. Agricultural produce is the most important of the commodities belonging to this class; but it also includes the produce of mines and of fisheries. In order to explain what is meant by an article necessarily becoming more expensive as its supply is increased, let it be supposed that a party of emigrants form a village, and that they select, as they naturally would, the most fertile ground available for their purpose. We will also suppose that this village consists of fifty persons, and that all the food which they require is raised on the fertile land immediately surrounding their settlement. In the course of a few years the population of the village increases from 50 to 150; it is therefore evident that the community requires three times as much food as it did when first it was formed. Where is this increased supply of food to come from? It is replied—by going a few miles out of the village there is abundance of fertile land from which the additional food can be supplied. This is quite true; for we have given the village the advantage of placing it in the midst of a fertile district. But the food which is raised a few miles out of the village will not be brought to market at so small a cost as that which grows close at hand. The cost of carriage must be paid for by the consumers. Suppose that wheat grown immediately on the confines of the village had been sold at 10s. a quarter; the corn raised on equally fertile ground at a few miles' distance could be grown at a similar cost; but the labor of conveying this corn to the place where it is required must be remunerated, and it may be supposed that the rate of remuneration is 9d. a quarter. When therefore the corn reaches the village its price is 10s. 9d. a quarter. The price of all the corn consumed in the village will therefore be raised; for those who own the land immediately joining the village will not continue to sell their corn at 10s. a quarter when corn in no way superior to theirs realizes 10s. 9d. In this example it has been supposed that the community is surrounded by an abundant supply of equally productive land, and that therefore when an increased supply of food is required the only additional cost incurred is the expense of carriage. But it is easy to perceive that the increased labor of obtaining an additional supply of food would be greatly augmented if it were necessary to resort to land not only less conveniently situated but also less fertile. Every quarter of corn grown on land of inferior productiveness might require 30 percent more capital and labor to produce it and bring it to market; if this were the case the price of corn throughout the community would be increased 30 percent.

There is yet another case to be considered, in which the additional supply of food could not be provided except at a much greater cost. Suppose that the village community were settled on a small island, or in a mountain valley shut in by rocks, where an extended area of cultivable land was not attainable. The additional supply of food which the increased population of such a village would require could only be obtained by improving the cultivation of the land already under the plow, by an increased application of labor and capital. It is however well known that after a certain point, even with the advantages of improved machinery and scientific farming, double the amount of capital and labor does not double the produce; and the cost of the increased quantity of food might very possibly be twice as much per quarter as that which was formerly required by the smaller population.

The growth of population tends to increase the price of food. From these examples it is seen that the increased demand for food caused by an increased population cannot be satisfied without increasing the cost of the production of food; in other words, an increase of population exerts a direct tendency to raise the price of agricultural produce. The supply must be made equal to the demand; the demand increases with the growth of population, and an increased supply cannot be obtained but at a greater cost. The tendency of the growth of population to increase the price of agricultural produce can be to some extent counteracted in two ways:

First. By the importation of agricultural produce from other countries.

Second. By improved agricultural machinery, and by the application of chemical discoveries, such as powerful manures.

The influence exerted by the first of these counteracting causes has in our country been very great. Notwithstanding a vast increase in our population since 1841,[1] the price of corn has not materially increased. The repeal of the corn laws in 1846 has rendered the existence of this increased population possible. The corn laws, by imposing a heavy duty upon all corn imported into this country, greatly checked the importation of food from foreign countries, and made the population of England mainly dependent on the supplies of corn that could be grown at home. Hence an increase in population exerted its full effect in raising the price of agricultural produce. If the corn laws had not been repealed the growth of population must have been checked; had it continued to increase corn must have risen to a famine price. One may form some estimate of the effect of increased population upon the price of food by considering those commodities which cannot be, to any considerable extent, imported. The price of milk, fresh butter and eggs has steadily and of late years rapidly increased; and if the population goes on increasing, there is no doubt that these commodities will get dearer still. The rise in the price of butcher's meat, which at one time threatened to be very great, has been checked by the successful importation of excellent fresh meat from America.

A summary of the laws governing the price of Agricultural Produce. The following is a brief summary of the causes which regulate the price of agricultural produce.

An equality must be effected between the demand and the supply. When the demand is in excess of the supply the equality cannot be restored, as with some other commodities, by withdrawing a corresponding portion of the demand. For the demand for the necessaries of life must always bear a proportion to the number of the population. The demand for such a commodity as bread does not vary in an inverse ratio with its price. People must either eat or die, whether bread is dear or cheap; the effect therefore of the price of bread upon the demand for it is very small, for people are obliged to relinquish every unnecessary expenditure before they diminish their demand for bread. It was said above that the demand for necessaries could not be withdrawn in the same manner as a demand for other commodities. This is true, it cannot be withdrawn in the same way; but it can be and is diminished by starvation and semi-starvation. But this means of reducing the demand necessarily diminishes the number of the population, so it still remains true that the demand for necessaries must always be proportionate to the number of the population. When, therefore, the demand is in excess of the supply, equality is restored, not by decreasing the demand, but by increasing the supply. In order to increase the supply resort must be had to less fertile or to less conveniently situated land. When this is done the additional quantity of food is raised at a greater expenditure of labor and capital; in other words, the cost of production is increased, and prices consequently rise. It is therefore seen that, as regards the necessaries of life, the demand does not depend on the price, but the price depends upon the demand; that is to say, the price depends, other things being equal, upon the number of the population. It should, however, be pointed out, that counteracting circumstances often prevent a rise in the price of food corresponding to the increase of the population. Free trade, for instance, and other agencies, have prevented a rise in the price of wheat at all commensurate with the increase of the population of England during the present century.

The productions of Mines and Fisheries. What has been stated with regard to agricultural produce is also true with regard to the produce of mines and fisheries. When an increased demand for fish takes place, the demand is satisfied by resorting to less productive or more distant fisheries; hence the cost of production (that is the labor and risk incident to production) is increased, and prices rise. The great rise which took place in the price of coal about 1872 may in great part be traced to similar causes. An extraordinary activity in the iron trade in the years 1871–2 caused a great increase in the demand for coal. This demand had to be satisfied by resorting to seams of coal which were less productive, and consequently more costly than those that were formerly sufficient to satisfy the demand. Hence the increased demand could not be met except at a largely increased cost. The sudden rise in price was not produced, as it seems sometimes to be supposed, by the increased wages paid to colliers; the rise in wages followed the rise in prices. The men took advantage of the exceptional activity of the trade to demand and obtain higher wages. The increase in the men's wages moreover only amounted to 2s. per ton of the coal raised; whereas the rise in price at the pit's mouth was more than 10s. per ton. The exceptionally large demand for coal began to fall off in 1873, and prices began to fall, consequently the seams of coal which were so poor that they only just provided the ordinary rate of wages and profits when coal was dear, could no longer be worked at a profit when prices fell; they were therefore gradually abandoned. A very poor seam of coal may yield a profit when the produce fetches 30s. a ton; but a fall to 25s. or 20s. a ton will turn this profit into a loss, and then the working of the seam will be discontinued.

The Laws which govern the Price of Manufactured Commodities. When illustrating the general theory of value the laws regulating the price of manufactured commodities were referred to; but it may be desirable more fully to explain their nature, for manufactured articles are those whose supply can be increased without increasing their cost of production. They therefore form the third of the classes into which commodities are divided in respect to their price.

It has been previously stated that the price of such commodities is governed by their cost of production, insofar as free competition exists among their producers. It is now necessary fully to explain of what elements their cost of production is composed. It may perhaps be thought that the price of manufacturing produce is governed by the same laws as those which regulate the price of agricultural and mining produce. For the materials of which manufactured commodities are made are always derived from the land. A piece of linen cloth is composed of flax; it may therefore be thought that as an increased supply of linen is produced, the cost of producing it must be augmented, because the raw material of which it is composed will gradually become more expensive. The price of the raw material no doubt forms a part of the price of manufactured commodities; but with most manufactures it does not form an important part. Take the instance of a piece of cotton cloth. The number of processes which the cotton goes through is so great that the price of the raw material forms but a very small part of the cost of producing the cotton cloth. The raw cotton is grown in America; it has to be packed on board ship, and conveyed across the ocean to Liverpool; when it arrives in England it goes through almost innumerable processes, carried on by different classes of laborers, all of whom have to be remunerated; the capital also which is required for carrying on these various processes must be replaced and rewarded by the ordinary rate of profit.

The principal Element of Cost of Production. It is therefore seen that the principal element in the cost of producing a manufactured commodity is labor; the abstinence of the capitalist is also an important component of the cost of production; the influence of the price of the raw material is in most cases of minor consideration as compared with the cost of labor and abstinence. The price realized by the commodity must be, as previously explained, such as to yield a sufficient inducement to the capitalist and the laborer to continue their exertions.

It very often happens that the cost of the production of manufactured commodities not only does not increase but actually diminishes when the supply is increased. When production is carried on on a large scale, many of the processes of manufacture can be economized. Steam power, in nearly all cases where it can be applied, effects an immense saving both of capital and labor. Unless, however, there is a large system of production steam power cannot be successfully introduced. Handloom weaving, for instance, could never have been superseded by steam power and machinery, if production on a large scale had not taken the place of production on a small scale. As a rule, the expenses of carrying on business do not increase in proportion to the quantity of business done. The same buildings can very often accommodate an increased number of workmen. The overlooker and the designer can superintend and direct the labor of a large number of workmen as well as that of a smaller number. The bookkeeping department does not require a proportionate increase of clerks and accountants when business transactions are doubled or trebled. It is also obviously much easier to have complete division of labor where production is carried on on a large scale. For instance, when the handloom was used, all the processes of weaving cloth were performed by one individual. Now each process is performed by a separate set of workers, and production is thereby greatly assisted. A small capitalist who carries on a limited trade cannot afford to purchase expensive machinery, because he would not be able to keep it in full work. There are some commodities for which there is a very limited demand, the cost of whose production would be greatly diminished if a largely increased supply were wanted. A remarkable instance of this is afforded by the manufacture of small rowing boats. A machine has been invented for the manufacture of these boats which would effect a reduction in their cost of 30 percent. The machine has not, however, been adopted by boatbuilders, for this reason; the machine works so rapidly that it would soon turn out more planks than are required for all the boats built in a year. If, therefore, a boatbuilder went to the expense of buying one of these machines he would most likely not require to keep it at work more than one month in the year. During the eleven remaining months the machine would be lying idle, and not returning any profit to its owner. This machine will therefore probably never be used unless the demand for boats should very largely increase; or unless all the boats required in several countries could be made by the same builder.

Cost of Labor to the Capitalist does not vary with the amount of Wages. It must be borne in mind that the cost of labor to the capitalist does not always vary with the amount of wages which he pays his men; it varies in proportion to the work done as compared with the wages given. For instance, it is well known that skilled, and therefore highly paid labor, is more remunerative in such a business as watchmaking or glassblowing than unskilled labor; the former is therefore less costly than the latter, although the wages of the unskilled workman may be only half as much as those of the skilled workman. When some railways were being made in France, it was found by Mr. Brassey, the great railway contractor, that it was to his advantage to bring over large numbers of English navvies; for although they received twice as large wages as the French navvies, they did more than twice as much work. The labor of the Englishman was therefore not so costly as that of the Frenchman, although the Englishman's wages were double those of the Frenchman.

There is another aspect in which the effect of the efficiency of labor may be considered. The increased efficiency of labor is capable of conferring a vast benefit upon the laborers themselves. Increased efficiency signifies that a given quantity of capital and labor becomes more productive of wealth. If, therefore, prices remain unchanged, the profits of capital and the wages of labor may both be increased by the increased efficiency of labor. Suppose that education increased the efficiency of the labor of the agricultural peasant. It might very possibly have this effect by making him more intelligent, more trustworthy and more sober. His employer could in this case increase his wages without decreasing his own profits and his landlord's rent, and without raising the price of agricultural produce.

The Profits of Capital. It will not be possible here to state the various agencies which produce the average rate of profit at different times and in different countries. The subject will be dwelled upon in a future section on the distribution of wealth. It is sufficient here to state that causes are constantly in operation which tend to make the interest of capital in all trades in the same country and at the same time approximate to an average. When capital appears permanently to realize higher profits in one trade than in another, these additional profits ought not in strict accuracy to be looked upon as profits of capital; they are either wages of labor, compensation for risk, for the disagreeableness of the occupation, or for its dishonorable reputation. When all these disturbing causes are removed, it will be found that the interest of capital tends to an equality.

The nature of capital has been already explained; it is now therefore sufficient to state that the profits of capital are the share of the wealth, produced by the joint agency of land, labor, and capital, which is allotted to capital. The amount of this reward differs at different times and in different nations. In some countries capitalists obtain a clear return of £10 a year upon every £100 which they invest in trade; besides what they receive as compensation for risk and as wages for superintendence. When this is the case the rate of interest is said to be 10 percent. In most countries the average rate of interest is much lower; in England it is about 3¼ percent.

The relations between Profits and Prices. It must always be remembered that the reward of the capitalist and of the laborer (i.e., their profits and wages) must be contained in the price of the commodity which they have combined to produce. This price must (if the manufacture is to be continued) be sufficient to yield to the capitalist and laborer the rate of profits and wages current in the trade at that time. If the price is less than this the laborer and capitalist would earn more by engaging in other industries, and the production of the commodity would be checked. Therefore any circumstance which raises the rate of profit current in a country, or which raises the rate of wages in any particular trade without increasing the efficiency of labor and capital, will cause a higher price to be paid for the commodity produced.

It will however be obvious on a brief consideration that the rate of profits and wages will be in the main dependent on the efficiency of a given exertion of capital and labor resulting in a large production of commodities. When this is the case cost of production is low, wages and profits are high, and prices may be low. It is thus seen that high profits do not always accompany high prices, nor low profits low prices. Suppose, for instance, that a village carpenter invents a machine which increases the productive power of his capital and labor 50 percent. Where he before made ten boxes or ten tables, he is now able to make, by the same expenditure of capital and labor, fifteen boxes or fifteen tables. It is evident that unless prices decline he will realize 50 percent more as a return to his capital and labor. His wages and his profits have both increased; and the cost of production has decreased. It is not, however, probable that he would be able permanently to retain the whole of the advantage of his invention. The increased supply of boxes, chairs, tables, etc., would ultimately cause a reduction of price. The demand, it has often been repeated, must be made equal to the supply. The supply is in this case increased 50 percent. It may be supposed that the supply was equal to the demand before this increase took place. The carpenter will therefore find it necessary to reduce the price of his manufactures, if he desires to find customers for them. He may perhaps find by experience that a reduction of 15 percent in the price is sufficient to sell all his stock. He therefore parts with this portion of the advantage produced by his invention, and retains an addition to his own wages and profits of 35 percent. In this case wages and profits are both increased, while the cost of production and ultimately prices are diminished.

In the case just investigated it has been supposed that the village carpenter who invents this machine has no rival, of his own trade, in his locality. But suppose there were three or four carpenters in the same village; they would as soon as possible procure similar machines; the supply of chairs, tables, etc. would be very largely increased. Each carpenter, in order to find purchasers, would try to undersell the others, and finally they might be induced to part with the whole of the advantage of the invention to their customers; the wages and profits of the carpenters would return to their former level, and prices would be reduced 50 percent. This example shows:

First. That when the efficiency of labor and capital are increased, wages and profits rise, and the cost of production is diminished.

Second. That when this increased efficiency takes place wages and profits may rise, simultaneously with a decrease in prices.

Third. That where free competition exists between capitalists on the one hand, and laborers on the other, the whole benefit arising from the increased efficiency of capital and labor is generally gained by the consumer. That is to say, that increased efficiency decreases prices, and does not permanently raise the wages of labor or the profits of capital.

It should be here pointed out that although increased efficiency generally operates in reducing the price of the particular article in question; and does not raise the money wages of labor or the profits of capital, yet if the article cheapened by the invention be one which enters into the consumption of laborers and capitalists, the real reward of labor and capital is increased; that is to say, the money distributed in wages and in profits has a greater purchasing power. If the article cheapened be boots, the wages of labor, though remaining at the same sum, would in reality be increased, because the same amount of money would exchange for an increased number of commodities. In the manner just indicated capitalists and laborers have benefited by the application of steam to industry. The advantage of the immense addition which is thus made to the efficiency of capital and labor could not be permanently retained by the laborers and capitalists in the form of a universal increase in wages or a higher general rate of profit. Competition of other laborers and capitalists prevented that. The ultimate benefit which they derived from the increased efficiency of labor and capital was in the consequent reduction in price of nearly all manufactured commodities. This point will be hereafter further explained.

A **summary of the effect of Demand and Supply on Prices.** The following is a brief summary of the manner in which the prices of the three classes of commodities above enumerated are acted upon by demand and supply. It must be borne in mind that the price in the case of all these commodities is adjusted in such a way as to equalize the demand with the supply.

In the case of the first class of commodities, those whose supply is absolutely limited, the supply is made equal to the demand by raising the price to such a point that the demand exceeding the supply is withdrawn.

In the case of the second class of commodities, whose supply cannot be increased without increasing cost of production, the demand (owing to the great proportion of this class being composed of the necessaries of life) cannot be greatly reduced: when therefore the demand is in excess of the supply, the supply must be increased. This cannot be done without increasing the cost of production, and in order to recompense this increased exertion of labor and capital, prices rise.

In the case of the third class of commodities, whose supply can be indefinitely increased without increasing their cost of production, when the demand is in excess of the supply, prices rise, and a portion of the demand is withdrawn; but this manner of equalizing the demand to the supply is only temporary; when the price of a commodity rises above what is necessary to provide the current rate of wages and profits to its producers, production is greatly stimulated. This increased production increases the supply, and prices fall; the adjustment of the supply to the demand ultimately taking place by means of an increased supply.

Having now investigated the causes which regulate the prices of the three classes into which commodities are divided, the next chapter will be devoted to an explanation of the value of money.

QUESTIONS ON CHAPTER III. *THE VALUE OF COMMODITIES*

1. Into what classes are commodities divided in relation to their value?
2. What is "cost of production"?
3. What are the principal elements of cost of production as stated by Mr. Mill?
4. What other definition has been given by Prof. Cairnes of cost of production?
5. What is the accurate explanation of the expression "that prices depend upon demand and supply"?
6. Give an illustration of the manner in which the adjustment of prices equalizes demand and supply.

7. Explain the manner in which the tendency is exerted to make the market price of a commodity approximate to a sum just sufficient to yield the current rate of wages and profits to the laborer and capitalist who produce it.

8. This approximation takes place only when the supply of the commodity can be increased. In what manner is the price of those commodities adjusted, the supply of which is absolutely limited?

9. What is "effectual demand"?

10. By what two qualities is every article characterized which has an exchange value?

11. Are these qualities always present in the same degree?

12. Give illustrations.

13. Which quality is the more active in determining the price of such a commodity as one of Raphael's pictures?

14. What are the principal of the commodities which become more expensive as their supply is increased?

15. Show, by an illustration, the operation of the causes by which an additional supply of food must be produced at a greater proportionate expenditure of capital and labor.

16. What causes a demand for an additional supply of food?

17. What circumstance therefore has a stronger tendency than any other to increase the price of food?

18. How is this tendency sometimes counteracted?

19. Mention some other commodities which are subject to the same laws as those which regulate the price of agricultural produce.

20. Name the last of the three classes into which commodities are divided in respect to their value.

21. Are the laws which govern the price of manufactured commodities the same as those which regulate the price of agricultural produce?

22. Explain the reason of the difference existing between them.

23. Illustrate the manner in which the price of manufactured commodities is sometimes decreased when the supply is augmented.

24. In what manner does efficiency of labor act upon cost of production?

25. What is the connection existing between wages, profits, cost of production, and prices?

26. Show by an illustration that, under certain circumstances, profits and wages can both be raised without increasing prices.

27. What practical conclusion can therefore be drawn respecting the connection of prices with the rate of profit and the wages of labor?

28. When there is a general increase of efficiency of labor and capital, in what way do laborers, capitalists and consumers benefit?

29. Give a summary of the laws which regulate the price of articles of vertu, agricultural produce, and manufactured commodities.

   (*a*) If the poor people took to eating grass, could the baker increase the size of his penny loaf?

   (*b*) What view of cost of production is taken by Hood in the lines: "Oh men with sisters dear, men with mothers and wives! It isn't linen you're wearing out, it's human creatures' lives."

   (*c*) If the cost of producing food remains the same, what will be the effect if the population of England goes on doubling itself every 60 years?

   (*d*) If a machine is invented that greatly facilitates the production of a particular commodity, do you think the inventor should take out a patent for it, and thus secure the advantages to himself instead of allowing, by the effect of competition, the consumers of the commodity to obtain all the benefit of the invention?

   (*e*) It has been said that the demand for a thing influences the price of it. Does the desire of a pauper to have a carriage influence the price of carriages? And if not, why not?

   (*f*) Supposing that all the members of my household decline to eat American meat, will the importation produce any effect on my butcher's bills?

   (*g*) Suppose meat were cheaper, and my butcher's bills were consequently reduced one-third, should I be permanently any better off, if about the same time I had nine people to keep instead of six?

CHAPTER FOUR

ON THE VALUE OF MONEY

IT IS NOT AT ALL AN UNCOMMON THING TO HEAR PEOPLE TALK ABOUT THE price of money. This expression is very often used respecting the rate of interest; when those who borrow money have to pay for the loan a large sum over and above the amount they receive, the price of money, or the rate of interest, is said to be high. When borrowers only pay a small sum for the use of the loan the price of money, or the rate of interest, is said to be low. It will, however, be shown that, apart from its commercial signification, the expression "the price of money" has no meaning whatever. It has been said in a former chapter that the value of a commodity is its exchange power, or the number of other commodities for which it will exchange. It was then explained that price is a particular case of value, that is, the value of a commodity estimated in money. When therefore the price of money is spoken of, in any other sense than that indicated above, it is equivalent to mentioning the value of money estimated in money. This is, of course a foolish expression; it might as well be said that the price of ten pounds was ten sovereigns, or that the price of a shilling was two sixpences. It is impossible to measure the value of a commodity by comparing it with itself.

The value of Money. The value of money is its exchange power: when money exchanges for a large quantity of other commodities, or in other words, when prices are low, the value of money is high;

when money exchanges for a small amount of other commodities, or in other words, when prices are high, the value of money is low.

The value of Money is regulated by the same laws as those which determine the value of other mineral produce. It is sometimes erroneously supposed that the value of money is invariable, because an ounce of gold can always be exchanged for the same amount of money. Whether prices are high, or whether they are low, an ounce of gold can always be exchanged at the Mint for £3. 17s. 10½d. Those who think that this fact proves the value of gold to be unalterable would also be likely to believe that the value of land is unchangeable, because an acre of land can always be divided into four plots of a quarter of an acre each. The fact that an ounce of gold will always exchange for £3. 17s. 10½d. only shows that an ounce of gold will divide into three sovereigns and that part of a sovereign which is represented by 17s. 10½d.

It must be borne in mind that the value of the precious metals is regulated in the same manner as the value of other mineral products. The value therefore of the precious metals is adjusted by an equalization of the demand with the supply. As the demand increases the value rises, and the production of an increased supply is also stimulated. If this increased supply is obtained from less productive sources, the cost of production will be increased and the value of the precious metals will be augmented. If however the increased supply is obtained by the discovery of more productive mines, the cost of production will be reduced and the value of the precious metals will diminish. The yield of silver from America has of recent years been enormously increased owing to the discovery of very productive mines. From the years 1849 to 1858, the yield of silver from American mines was of the value of £10,000 per annum. About the year 1861 the yield began largely to increase, and in the year 1873 it had reached the enormous value of £7,150,000. This and some other circumstances have caused a serious fall in the value or purchasing power of silver, and is occasioning great anxiety and inconvenience to those countries which, like India, have silver for their standard currency. It does not affect the value of the English currency, because our silver coins are merely tokens; twenty shillings have never contained a value of silver equivalent to the value of the gold contained in a sovereign. Gold is our standard currency, and is the only legal tender for the payment of debts of more than 40s. in amount. The value of silver has already declined ⅙ or nearly 17 percent. That is to say that 6 rupees can now only purchase the same amount of commodities as could formerly be purchased for 5 rupees. The inconvenience to the government of India arises from the fact that while their expenditure for stores etc. must be largely increased, the principal item of their revenue, the rent of land, is fixed by law in pecuniary amount and cannot be increased.

The circumstances which influence the Demand for Gold and Silver. It has been previously explained that the demand for a commodity is regulated by its value. To this rule money is no exception. To carry on a given amount of business about fifteen times more silver would be needed than gold: and why? Because silver is fifteen times less valuable. The quantity of money required in any country will depend partly on the cost of its production, and partly on the rapidity of its circulation. The principal use to which gold and silver are devoted is the formation of money; but they are also used in many processes of art and manufacture. The demand which each country has for gold and silver therefore depends on their value; on the national wealth and population; the number of times commodities are bought and sold for money; and the activity of the arts and manufactures in which gold and silver are required.

When it is said that the demand for money depends on the national wealth, it must not be supposed that the wealth of a nation can be accurately measured by the amount of gold and silver which it keeps in circulation. The wealth of an individual is not measured by the quantity of money which passes through his hands. He uses various substitutes for money, such as cheques and banknotes, for nearly all his larger payments; but he is obliged to use money for his smaller payments; for paying servants and laborers, and for defraying daily expenses, such as cab fares and hotel bills. It is therefore seen that, though the amount of money used by an individual is not by any means a measure of his wealth, still his demand for money generally bears some proportion to his wealth; as his wealth increases he employs more servants, or more laborers, he takes longer and more expensive journeys, and his daily expenses probably increase.

As it is with an individual so is it with a nation. The demand for money is not an accurate measure of national wealth, but it always bears some proportion to the wealth and population of a country. Thus, in a country of twenty million inhabitants, a very far larger number of persons are in receipt of money wages than in a country containing ten million inhabitants. The increased demand for money has not however been proportionate to the increase of population and wealth in this country during the last twenty years. This is doubtless owing to the facilities of banking which now so largely prevail. An immense quantity of buying and selling is transacted every day in England by means of cheques without the use of a single coin of any kind. It has been said that in proportion to the extent of its commerce England employs less actual coin than any other country. The way in which cheques obviate the use of gold and silver will be explained in detail in the chapter on "Credit and its influence on prices"; the way in which cheques take the place of coin, at the moment when they are used is however so obvious as not to require any explanation. Formerly large business payments were made by means of money. Farmers who came to market to buy or sell corn or stock always expected to pay and to be paid in money. In this way on a market day in a country town thousands of pounds would change hands. But in these large transactions the use of money is now entirely dispensed with. Farmers bring their chequebooks to market; the use of money is not required except for the purpose of paying the expenses incurred on the journey. Although therefore the demand for money bears some proportion to the wealth and population of a country, yet the proportion is not fixed and definite, for it is liable to alterations with every extension of the credit system.

The demand for the precious metals is also influenced, to a very great degree, by the number of times commodities are bought and sold for money. If for instance a piece of linen after it is manufactured is sold for money to a wholesale dealer, who in his turn sells it again for money to a retail shopman, who sells it to a lady to make shirts for a missionary basket, the same piece of linen is exchanged for money four times before it is put to its ultimate purpose. It is evident that such a series of transactions must require a far greater quantity of money than would be used if the cloth were sold by the manufacturer to the consumer. It may here be remarked that it has become customary to dispense with the use of money in large trade transactions. The wholesale dealer would in all probability now pay the manufacturer with a cheque or with a bill of exchange, and the retail tradesman would pay the wholesale dealer in the same way; by these means the quantity of money in circulation is greatly economized. The example, however, shows how the demand for gold and silver in each country is partly regulated by the number of times commodities are bought and sold before they are used.

It is hardly necessary to enter into an explanation of the manner in which the demand for gold and silver is affected by the quantity of those metals used in arts and manufactures. It has been said that the value of gold and silver is regulated by the same laws as the value of other mineral produce; any circumstance therefore which causes an increased use of the precious metals in arts and manufactures will, if other things remain unchanged, cause an increased demand for gold and silver, and this increased demand would cause their value to rise.

Illustrations showing the action of increased Demand and Supply upon the Value of Money. In order to investigate more fully the action of demand upon the value of gold and silver, let it be supposed that no substitutes for money, such as banknotes and bills of exchange, exist. Let it be further supposed that the supply of gold and silver cannot be augmented by fresh discoveries or by foreign importations. These suppositions reduce the problem to great simplicity. We will now take the case of a country whose inhabitants carry on their commercial transactions entirely by gold and silver coin, the amount of which they have no means of increasing. Let it be supposed that in such a community a great increase in the production of wealth takes place, that all manufactures are doubled, and that population increases. In such a case the same amount of money is used to carry on twice as much buying and selling; general prices must therefore have declined one-half, or, in other words, the value of gold and silver has doubled. Let us take another illustration. It may be supposed that the trade, population, and manufactures of a community are stationary; and that all payments are made in money. The money which such a community keeps in circulation may be said to be £10,000,000. Owing to the discovery of gold or silver mines, or to foreign importations, the quantity of money in circulation is increased by £2,000,000. The same quantity of commodities is bought and sold the same number of times; the same number of people receive wages; but the circulation of the country is increased by one-fifth. Under these circumstances a corresponding rise must take place in wages and in prices, the value or the exchange power of gold having decreased 20 percent. This example shows that, in the absence of counteracting circumstances, every increase in the quantity of gold and silver in circulation diminishes the value or purchasing power of gold. The first example proved that if wealth were increased without a corresponding increase in the amount of money in circulation, the value or purchasing power of gold must increase. Increased prices do not indicate increased prosperity.

It is perhaps hardly necessary to point out that the increase of wealth on the one hand, and the increase of the circulation on the other, never actually produce their full effect upon the value of gold and silver. In the above examples it was necessary to assume the absence of counteracting circumstances, which in reality are always present. In the first example it was supposed that a great increase of manufactures and population took place without any increase in the quantity of gold and silver in circulation. Hence it was said that the value of money would be greatly increased; but when the value of money is augmented, the supply is stimulated; and with the growth of commerce various substitutes for money are nearly always adopted. Such counteracting circumstances as these usually suffice to prevent great and sudden fluctuations in the value of money.

The effect of the recent Gold Discoveries. In the second example a great augmentation of the money in circulation was supposed to take place, without any increase in population or wealth. A very great increase in the amount of money in circulation has taken place since the year 1850, when the great discoveries of gold were made in Australia and California. Previous to 1850, the annual yield of gold from all sources was about £6,000,000, about £4,000,000 of which was sent to England. The gold fields of Australia and California have had an average annual yield of £10,000,000 each, about £14,000,000 of which has each year been sent to England. The supply of gold annually sent to this country has therefore been more than trebled since the year 1850. It was at first predicted, by all the most competent authorities, that this immense increase in the annual supply of gold, would cause the value of gold rapidly to decline, and produce a marked rise in general prices. These predictions, however, have not been fulfilled; indeed it was for some time doubted, whether the recent gold discoveries had produced any effect on general prices. After the most careful investigation, it has been estimated that the value of gold has decreased, since 1850, by about 15 percent. This comparatively slight decrease bears no proportion to the increase in the supply of gold. It is therefore interesting to inquire what has become of all this additional gold. It is remarkable that simultaneously with the discovery of the gold fields of Australia and California five circumstances took place which exercised a great influence in absorbing the additional supply of gold:

First. A great development of commerce, consequent on the growth of our railway system, commenced about that time.

Second. Free Trade had just begun to cause a great increase in manufactures and population.

Third. Owing to a failure of the silk crops of France and Italy, we began to import large quantities of silk from China, in return for which the Chinese would accept nothing but silver, whereas France and Italy had accepted our manufactured commodities.

Fourth. Large quantities of silver were exported to India, to pay wages, and defray other expenses consequent on the formation of railroads in that country.

Fifth. France and, more recently, Germany have adopted a gold coinage, in the place of their old silver coinage. This has absorbed a large quantity of gold and set free a corresponding value of silver, with the consequence of checking the fall in the value of gold and greatly increasing the fall in the value of silver.

The first two of these circumstances need little explanation; it has been previously stated that any circumstance which produces an increased amount of buying and selling, or which causes a larger number of people to be hired for weekly wages, will, if other things remain unchanged, increase the value of gold, and create a decline in general prices and in wages. Hence it may be inferred that, if the development of our railway system and the adoption of free trade had not happened to be nearly simultaneous with the gold discoveries in Australia and California, there would have been a fall in general prices, and money wages would have declined.

The third and fourth of these circumstances need more explanation. The export of specie to India and China was chiefly confined to silver; it might therefore seem that this export would not produce any effect on the value of gold. The fact however is that the greater part of the silver thus exported has been obtained from the coinage of other countries, such as France; the silver five-franc piece was formerly in very general use in France, but this coin has now been to a large extent superseded by the gold five-franc piece. Great numbers of the silver five-franc pieces have been bought up and exported to India and China, and their place has been taken by the gold coin. Some idea of the immense flow of silver to India and China in recent years may be gathered from the fact that in 1847 we purchased 55,000,000 lbs. of tea whereas we in 1878 purchased 204,000,000 lbs. Formerly only a small quantity of silk was imported from China; we now import more than 4,000,000 lbs. of silk. Considerably less than half of these imports has been exchanged for our manufactured commodities. In 1876 the value of our imports from China was

£14,921,000; while the value of the articles of commerce which we exported to China was in the same year £4,611,000. On the mere consideration of the exchange of commodities between England and China, there was therefore a balance against England of £10,310,000, which had to be defrayed by the export of specie to that amount to China. This state of trade between England and China is not special or exceptional. Our imports from China are constantly and largely in excess of our exports to that country, in consequence of the reluctance of the Chinese government to admit our manufactures; this circumstance creates a constant drain of money towards the East. In the same way the value of our exports to India is constantly lower by many millions, than the value of our imports from that country. In 1876 the difference amounted to more than sixteen millions sterling. The railways and other public works which have been carried out in India have absorbed an immense amount of English capital. It has been estimated that in seven years £43,000,000 of English capital were expended upon Indian railways alone. These circumstances have caused a very large quantity of money to be sent every year from England to the East.[1]

These facts are sufficient to account for the slight decrease in the value of gold as compared with the vast increase in the annual supply. It should be borne in mind that the five circumstances above mentioned, as having produced the absorption of the new supplies of gold, were quite independent of the gold discoveries; the development of commerce in England, the growth of population and wealth consequent on Free Trade, and the accompanying expansion of trade to the East, would have taken place whether the gold fields had been discovered or not. They were not in any sense produced by the augmentation of the supply of gold. Had the gold discoveries been made at a time when commerce and population were stationary, no general benefit would have been reaped by any countries except those actually in possession of the gold mines; and the benefit to these countries it must be remembered consists principally in increasing their purchasing power. Australia and California, as Prof. Cairnes has pointed out, have benefited by the gold which they possess insofar as they have parted with it by purchasing the commodities produced by other countries. The gold discoveries have however been of great service to the whole mercantile world because they increased the supply of the circulating medium just at the time when the growth of commerce made the increase most needful. It would have been a great commercial misfortune and embarrassment if the gold discoveries had taken place at a time when trade was stationary; the terms of all monetary contracts would have been disturbed by the alteration in the value of gold. Everyone would probably have had more money, but the purchasing power of money would have decreased. As previously stated, this inconvenience is now actually being suffered in India, in consequence of the fall in the value of silver. It must not be forgotten that if general prices are doubled, a man who formerly had a pound a week is no better off if he is now in receipt of two pounds a week; because the two pounds will only exchange for the same quantity of commodities that could formerly be obtained for one pound. M. Bastiat's illustration, at the end of the second chapter of this Section, demonstrates the truth of this assertion. If, in a game of cards, the stake remain unchanged, it matters little how many counters are used to represent the stake. The fewer the counters, the greater the value they represent; the greater the number of the counters, the less is their exchange power.

QUESTIONS ON CHAPTER IV. *THE VALUE OF MONEY*

1. What is the meaning of the phrase "price of money"?
2. Why in an economic sense is such an expression meaningless?
3. What is the value of money? Why is it sometimes erroneously supposed that the value of money is invariable?
4. Into what class of commodities must money be placed in relation to its value?
5. How is the value of the precious metals regulated?
6. What circumstances have occasioned a fall in the value or purchasing power of silver?
7. Name the principal circumstances which produce a demand for gold and silver.

8. Explain the manner in which the demand for money varies with national wealth and population.

9. By what means is the use of money, in large commercial transactions, usually dispensed with? Give an illustration.

10. Illustrate the manner in which the demand for money is increased when commodities are bought and sold for money many times, previous to their consumption.

11. Show by an illustration the action of increased demand upon the value of money.

12. Show by an illustration the action of increased supply upon the value of money.

13. Why do the results described in these examples never actually occur?

14. What circumstances generally counteract the effect of increased demand for gold and silver?

15. What has been the effect of the recent gold discoveries upon the value of money?

16. Enumerate the circumstances which have caused the decrease in the value of gold to be comparatively so slight.

17. Describe the action of these circumstances on the demand for gold.

18. What circumstances have rendered necessary a large annual export of silver from England to China?

19. Were the gold discoveries the cause of the increased trade and population of England?

20. What would have been the result had the gold discoveries been unaccompanied by an increase of wealth and population?

    (a) Suppose a wealthy millionaire desired to confer a benefit upon the inhabitants of some island that had no commercial relations with the outside world, would he accomplish his object by doubling the amount of money possessed by each of the islanders?

    (b) If population and commerce increased so that twice as many people were receiving wages, and twice as much buying and selling took place, what would be the effect on general prices and wages, supposing that the supply of money remained the same?

(c) If you could choose which of two Australian vessels should be lost, one laden with gold or one containing a corresponding value of wool and corn, which would you select?

(d) Would the wealth of England have been increased if the country had contained gold mines, instead of our iron and coal?

SECTION THREE

THE DISTRIBUTION OF WEALTH— INTRODUCTORY REMARKS

WEALTH IS DIVIDED INTO RENT, WAGES AND PROFITS. IN A PREVIOUS section on the Production of Wealth it was stated that the three agents of Production were Land, Labor, and Capital. It is therefore evident that Wealth is distributed between those who respectively own these agents of production, i.e., between the Landlord, the Laborer, and the Capitalist. The share allotted to the Landlord is termed Rent; that possessed by the Laborer is called Wages, while that belonging to the Capitalist is termed Profits. Wealth is therefore divided into three parts, viz. the Rent of Land, the Wages of Labor, and the Profits of Capital. In the following chapters the proportion which these three parts bear to each other will be pointed out, and the circumstances will be explained which cause an increase in one and a corresponding decrease in another. It will for instance be shown why a decline in general profits causes an increased amount to be paid as rent. This and many other interesting economic problems will easily be solved by those who rightly understand the laws which govern the distribution of wealth.

Rent, Wages and Profits are in various countries owned by different combinations of persons. In the case of agricultural industry Rent, Wages and Profits are nearly always in this country allotted to three distinct classes, viz. Landlords, Laborers and Capitalists. It must however be borne in mind that in other countries different modes of distribution prevail. In many parts of the continent the same individuals frequently possess all three of the agents of production. Land, Labor and Capital being in this case provided by one person called a peasant proprietor, he derives all the wealth which they are capable of producing, viz. Rent, Wages and Profits. In Ireland and in India labor and capital are in many cases provided by the same individual, who is a peasant tenant. In this case the tenant can fairly claim both wages and profits as his own, the rent only being the due of another person. From these examples it is seen that, in different countries, Land, Labor and Capital are owned by different combinations of persons, or, in other words, different tenures of land prevail.

QUESTIONS ON THE INTRODUCTORY REMARKS ON SECTION III

1. Into what shares is wealth divided, and to what productive agents do these shares correspond?
2. Are these shares always owned by different persons?
3. Mention some of the modes prevailing in different countries of distributing these shares.

CHAPTER ONE

The Rent of Land

A DEFINITION OF RENT. RENT IS THAT SHARE OF WEALTH WHICH IS claimed by the owners of land; it is the price which is paid to them for the use of their land. The rent of land is regulated in some countries by custom, and in others, as in England, by competition. The regulation of rent by competition means that, subject to certain conditions, the landlord will let his land to the farmer who offers him the best price for it. When rents are determined in this way there is virtually a bargain between landlord and tenant, just as there is between the buyer and seller of any ordinary commodity.

It is proposed first to explain the principles which determine the rent of land as regulated by competition, and then briefly to describe some of the tenures which are controlled by custom. It is unnecessary in this place to enquire how the owners of land originally came into possession of that which neither they nor any other persons have assisted to produce. It is sufficient to recognize that the land is in the possession of certain individuals, and the conclusions arrived at in this section will be based on this recognition. Rent is the effect of an appropriated natural monopoly. Land being absolutely limited in amount and the demand for it being very general, the owners of land can nearly always obtain a rent for it. "The reason why landowners are able to require rent for their land, is that it is a commodity which many want, and which no one can obtain but from them" (Mill's *Principles of Political Economy*, Vol. I p. 505).

A further analysis of the nature of Rent. The rent of agricultural land is regulated by two circumstances: the fertility of the soil, and the convenience of situation. When either of these conditions is altogether absent land can command no rent. Thus no one will pay rent for land which is so barren that the produce yielded by it is insufficient to remunerate the capital and labor expended in its cultivation. On the other hand, the most fertile land sometimes yields no rent, on account of the inconvenience of the situation in which it is placed. Large tracts of land in America and in Australia are in this condition; they are far removed from the great centers of population; roads, railways and water carriage, all being absent, there is no means of disposing of the abundant crops which the land is capable of producing. Such land as this consequently yields no rent. Some land of great natural fertility, situated most conveniently for the disposal of the produce, yields no rent; because the crops are either wholly destroyed or greatly injured by swarms of hares and rabbits. The rent of a very large proportion of the land of England is reduced in consequence of the damage done to the crops by ground game. The loss arising from this cause is not borne by the owner of the land only; it is also felt by the entire nation, which suffers a loss similar to that which it would have to bear if the natural fertility of the soil were reduced to an extent corresponding to the damage done by the hares and rabbits. The farmer may be compensated by reduction of his rent; but the consumers of agricultural produce have to give an increased price for it, in consequence of the diminution of the production.

Land in all countries varies greatly in fertility and in convenience of situation, and the rent of land, where rent is regulated by competition, varies in exact proportion with the productiveness[1] of the soil. If, for instance, there are two farms, one of which, owing to its superior productiveness, yields a much larger return to capital and labor than the other, the rent of the more productive farm will exceed that of the less productive farm by an amount exactly equaling the pecuniary value of the advantages of the first farm over those of the second farm. But it may still be asked "What determines the amount of rent paid by the two farms? It is quite evident that the more productive farm will pay a higher rent than that paid by the less productive farm, but what determines the rent of the latter?" In answering this question it will be necessary to explain Ricardo's theory of rent.

Ricardo's theory of Rent. The rent of the less productive farm is determined by the pecuniary value of the excess of its productiveness over that of the worst land in cultivation which pays only a nominal rent. This is a short statement of Ricardo's theory of rent, which we will now proceed to prove. In every country there is some land so barren or so inconveniently situated that the produce yielded by it is only sufficient to pay the wages of the laborers who till it, and to yield the ordinary rate of profit to the farmer. This land can obviously pay no rent, for if it did pay rent the cultivator would not receive the ordinary rate of profit upon his capital. The land would therefore cease to be cultivated if rent were exacted, for men will not continue to employ their capital in an occupation which yields less than the ordinary rate of profit.

The margin of cultivation. The rent of any particular land is therefore determined by the excess of its produce over that yielded by the least productive land in cultivation which pays no rent. This land is described by Ricardo as being upon the margin of cultivation, because land of still inferior productiveness, though free from rent, would not yield the ordinary rate of profit to the cultivator if agricultural prices remained unchanged. This leads to the second part of the explanation of Ricardo's theory.

The position of the margin of cultivation is determined by the price of agricultural produce. It is evident that the productiveness of the land on the margin of cultivation varies greatly at different times and in different countries. The price of agricultural produce is determined by the cost at which the most costly portion is raised; or, in other words, by the position in the scale of productiveness of the margin of cultivation. The questions therefore remain to be decided, "What determines the position in the scale of productiveness of the cultivated land that pays no rent?" and "Why would land which is on the margin of cultivation in Australia yield a large rent if it were in England?" A consideration of the price of agricultural produce furnishes the answer to both these questions. The position of the margin of cultivation is determined in all countries by the price of agricultural produce. Where agricultural produce is cheap the margin of cultivation is high, as it is in Australia, where the cultivation of none but highly productive land is profitable. As agricultural produce becomes dearer the margin of cultivation descends; because it then becomes profitable to cultivate soils of inferior productiveness. The truth of this assertion may be made evident by an illustration. Suppose that the price of agricultural produce suddenly rose one-third. The returns of farmers would be increased by a corresponding amount. The profits of farmers would then greatly exceed the average rate. But the competition of other traders would prevent farmers from permanently appropriating exceptionally large profits. The farms would consequently be let at increased rents. The land, formerly on the margin of cultivation, would now yield rent and the margin of cultivation would consequently descend.

A very striking example of the fact that the margin of cultivation varies from year to year, even with slight changes in the price of agricultural produce, may be seen on Salisbury Plain. Some of the land there is so barren that it does not pay a farmer to cultivate it unless the price of agricultural produce is high. When therefore prices are high some of the most barren land is cultivated, and the thin crops raised upon it remunerate the farmer for the capital and labor expended upon it. But when prices decline this land ceases to be cultivated, because the sale of the produce would not give a fair return to capital and labor. In a previous chapter the great rise in the price of coal which took place about 1872 was referred to; and it was then shown that this rise in price caused seams of coal to be worked at a profit which were so comparatively unproductive that they had to be abandoned when prices fell. The margin of cultivation (if this expression may be used in reference to a mine) declined when prices rose, and returned to its normal condition when the era of exceptionally high prices came to an end.

An increase of population increases the price of agricultural produce. It must be borne in mind that a lowering of the margin of cultivation can be produced only by an increase in the price of agricultural produce, because increased prices are necessary to render the cultivation of land below the margin of cultivation profitable. It has previously been pointed out that no circumstance is so potent in producing an augmentation of the price of agricultural produce as an increased demand for it, consequent on an increase in the population. An increase in the population necessarily implies an increased demand for agricultural produce. This increased demand raises the price, and it therefore becomes profitable to cultivate land of inferior productiveness to that formerly on the margin of cultivation. Hence an increase in population, causing an increased demand for agricultural produce, raises its price and produces a lowering of the margin of cultivation.

The increase of population raises the rent of land in two ways. In the first place, by stimulating the demand for agricultural produce it increases the value of it; and in the second place, in consequence of the lowering of the margin of cultivation, the share of the produce allotted to the landlord as rent is increased. For rent has been defined as the difference in value between the productiveness of any particular land, and that of the worst land in cultivation which pays no rent. Hence, when the margin of cultivation is lowered, this difference becomes greater and the rent of all land is increased. Let it be supposed that the value of the productiveness of some particular farm is represented by the number 100, and that the value of the productiveness of the land on the margin of cultivation is represented by 30. Then the rent of the first farm is represented by the number 70; but if the margin of cultivation is lowered so that the value of the productiveness of the worst land in cultivation which pays no rent is represented by 20, then the rent of the first farm becomes equal to a sum represented by the number 80.

A brief recapitulation of Ricardo's theory. The rent of any particular land is the difference between its productiveness, and the productiveness of the worst land in cultivation which pays no rent, that is, the land on the margin of cultivation. Any circumstance therefore which causes the margin of cultivation to descend increases rent, because it increases the difference between the productiveness of any particular land and that of the worst land in cultivation which pays no rent. The margin of cultivation is determined by the price of agricultural produce. The price of agricultural produce is determined by the demand for it, or, in other words, by the number of the population. Hence an increase in population exerts a powerful influence to increase rents.

There is a certain antagonism of interest between the owners of land and the consumers of agricultural produce. From Ricardo's theory of rent may be deduced the supposition that in some respects there is an antagonism of interest between the owners of land and other classes of the community. The increase of population exerts a powerful influence to increase rents; but if carried beyond a certain point it is disastrous to the general interests of the community. If it were not for the fact that the rates for the relief of the poor are to a very great extent a charge on land, this antagonism of interest would be much more powerful than it is. If the landlords were relieved from the cost of pauperism it would be actually advantageous to the pecuniary interests of the owners of the soil that people should marry recklessly, and bring large families into existence, so that population might be increased and rents raised. Regarded from this point of view, it is a wise precaution which has entailed on landlords the disagreeable as well as (to them) agreeable results of overpopulation. If landlords were relieved from bearing the cost of pauperism they would really grow rich on the improvidence of the poor. The very same circumstance which produced the increased wealth of the one class would deepen the misery and degradation of the other. Hence while the landlord was becoming more and more wealthy, the struggle for existence among the very poor would become more and more intense. The tendency of this antagonism of interest is to a great extent counterbalanced by the cost of pauperism; and there are fortunately many other respects in which the interests of the owners of land and those of the general community are identical.

In some respects the Interests of Landlord, Capitalist, and Laborer, are identical. Notwithstanding that increased pauperism and increased rents arise from the same cause, it does not follow that the interests of landowners and of other classes are necessarily opposed under all circumstances. On the contrary, the interests of the landlord, the capitalist, and the laborer, are in some respects the same. All are interested in rendering land, capital, and labor, as productive as possible. It is conceivable that some agencies may vastly increase the productive power of land, labor, and capital; in this case the share of wealth allotted to each might be increased, because there would be more to distribute as rent to the landlord, profits to the capitalist, and wages to the laborers. A few years ago the wages paid to agricultural laborers in the South of England were so low, and at the same time the prices of food were so comparatively high, that it was contended that the efficiency of the laborer was very materially reduced. The laborer was habitually underfed, and unsuitably clothed, he became prematurely old and feeble; this being so, many who knew intimately what his daily life was, asserted that if he were a slave or a cart horse it would serve the pecuniary interests of his owner to feed, house and clothe him better than he could afford to feed, house and clothe himself upon his wages. It was therefore argued that if the laborer received higher wages, his labor would become more efficient and he would consequently be a more valuable servant to his employer. The improvement in the laborers' condition which has lately taken place, did not however proceed from the enlightened self-interest of their employers. It was due to a combination of causes among which may be mentioned, First, the great fall in the price of provisions consumed by the laborers such as cheese and bacon, owing to the recent great importation of these things from America. This raised the daily standard of comfort of the entire class. Secondly, the gradual spread of education awakened the agricultural laborer to the fact that he was worse off than other laborers; he became discontented with wages at 9s. a week; railways and steamships gave him (materially speaking) the power to move to places where his labor would be better paid; the energy and enterprise which were the result of education gave him the moral power which the move required. Until a few years ago the agricultural laborers were practically excluded from the influence of competition. They were too ignorant and too timid to leave their homes in search of better paid employment. They were almost as incapable of independent action as the sheep and cattle they tended in the field. Now however this state of things has come to an end; there is a constant flow of population out of the agricultural counties into the manufacturing counties. It is perhaps too soon at present to say what the effect of this change will be on rent and on the profits of the farmers; it may however be confidently hoped, that, when the present rather transitional condition of things is over, all the three classes engaged in agriculture will benefit from the improvement in the intelligence and material comfort of the laborer. One fact may be mentioned in support of the reasonableness of this expectation. In Scotland and in Northumberland, the laborers have long been in a position very greatly superior to the laborers in the South of England; they are better educated, better housed and better paid; and not only are rents higher and the general condition of agriculture more satisfactory, but the labor bill on farms of a similar size and nature is actually less in those districts where wages are high than in those where wages are low. The labor bill of two farms of 380 acres, each requiring the same kind of labor, the one in Aberdeenshire and the other in Norfolk, have lately been compared; the Scotch laborers were paid 20s. a week, the Norfolk laborers 14s., yet the labor bill for the year was only £510 in Aberdeenshire compared with the £800 in Norfolk. The superior intelligence and energy of the laborer thus more than compensated the Scotch farmer for the higher rate of wages he was paying.

Population not a measure of National Prosperity. There are a vast number of economic problems which will be solved with perfect readiness by those who have a thorough grasp of Ricardo's theory of rent. A right understanding of this theory and of the proposition enunciated in Section I that a demand for commodities is not a demand for labor, will enable the student to detect and avoid some of the most common fallacies, which are often propounded as if they were self-evident truths. Such, for instance, as the statement so often either expressed, or implied in the newspapers and elsewhere, that the prosperity of all countries is accurately measured by the growth of their population—that in proportion as population increases, national prosperity also increases. This statement is, no doubt, within certain limits true, in a country like Australia, where there is abundance of fertile land, and where consequently the necessaries of life are very cheap. In such a country an increase of population augments the national wealth because an additional supply of labor is wanted to develop its great natural resources. But in some countries, such as India, an immense increase has taken place in the population, without a corresponding increase in wealth; the standard of comfort of the population has been lowered and vast numbers are constantly living just on the verge of pauperism and starvation. The people have no reserve of any kind and the failure of a crop immediately brings the pinch of want; they cannot meet bad times by giving up luxuries in order to buy necessaries; they have no luxuries; they have no cheaper kind of food to which they can resort; they are already at the bottom of the scale of human existence and to fall any lower means actual famine. It is obvious that in a country in such a situation as this, increase of population is in itself no indication of increased prosperity.

Rent does not increase the price of Agricultural produce. One of the most important conclusions deduced from Ricardo's theory is, that rent does not form a part of the price of agricultural produce; or, in other words, that agricultural produce would be no cheaper if all rents were remitted. We have seen that the price of agricultural produce is determined by the position of the margin of cultivation. The price of the produce must be such as to remunerate the capital and labor expended in tilling the worst land in cultivation which pays no rent. If prices were less, this land would cease to be cultivated, and the margin of cultivation would rise. But this cannot take place because the demand for agricultural produce would not be diminished by the remission of rents, and therefore as large a quantity of agricultural produce would be required as before; and, as previously stated, the demand for agricultural produce determines the position of the margin of cultivation.

The rent of land, regulated by competition and consisting of the excess of its return above the return of the worst land in cultivation, is called the rack rent.

One of the objections sometimes urged against Ricardo's theory is, that there can be no cultivated land rent free, as all farmers have to pay rent. It is no doubt true that there are few farms entirely composed of land which is so unproductive that it yields no rent; but many farms contain portions of such land, and though the rent may be reckoned upon the total number of acres of which the farm is composed, the rent would not be decreased if that land were subtracted which yields only sufficient produce to give the ordinary rate of profit to the cultivator, and to pay the wages of the labor expended in its cultivation. It is also objected to Ricardo's theory that farmers and landlords know nothing about it and do not regulate the rent of land in accordance with it. This is something like saying that the discoveries of anatomists must be wrong because most people live all their lives without knowing how their bodies are put together. People can eat what agrees with them without knowing anything of the process of digestion, and they can pay or receive a rack rent without ever having heard of Ricardo's theory.

The influence of custom on Rents. Throughout this chapter it has been assumed that rents are entirely regulated by competition. In England and Scotland this is almost invariably the case, but in most countries custom has a powerful influence in regulating rents. In some parts of Italy and France, for instance, a tenure prevails, called the metayer tenure, in which the produce of the soil is divided in a certain fixed proportion between the owner of the land and the cultivator. This proportion is usually one-half, but in some districts the owner of the land receives as much as two-thirds. The proportion allotted to the landlord is fixed by custom, and not by competition. Custom also regulates what part of the capital necessary for tilling the soil shall be provided by the landlord. In some places he supplies all the stock, implements and seed, which the cultivation of the land requires; in other districts the landlord furnishes the cattle and the seed, and the laborer provides the implements. The customs seem to be quite arbitrary, and are controlled by no fixed rule. Political economy cannot therefore define what circumstances determine the proportion in which the produce of a farm is distributed between the metayer tenant and his landlord. It will, however, be useful to consider the influence of the metayer system on the rent.

The influence of the metayer system on Rent. In those cases where rents are regulated by custom rather than by competition, the landlords are compelled to sacrifice some part of what may be called the economic rent as defined by Ricardo's theory. In Tuscany, for instance, the metayer rent is two-thirds of the produce, on soils of all degrees of productiveness. Now it is evident that if one-third of the produce of the least productive farm in Tuscany is sufficient to remunerate the cultivator for his capital and labor, one-third of the produce of the most productive farm in Tuscany must be more than sufficient to give the same rate of wages and interest to its cultivator. Under the metayer system the tenant shares with the landlord the advantage arising from the superior productiveness of the soil. Under the rack rent or competition system all the surplus which remains after paying wages to labor and the current rate of profit to the farmer, is claimed by the landlord as rent, so that tenants do not reap any permanent advantage from the superior productiveness of their farms. Under the metayer system the cultivator obtains some part of this surplus, he therefore possesses a beneficial interest in the productiveness of the soil. It is probable that this fact exercises a powerful influence in stimulating his industry, and the metayer tenure, though disadvantageous to landlords, may be beneficial to the general community. The economic defect of the metayer system is that it tends to prevent the expenditure of capital in permanent improvements. For instance, a metayer farm might want draining;

the landlord would know that if he provided the necessary capital for drainage the farm would be more productive, but that he would not be able to obtain more than one-half or two-thirds of its increased productiveness. Similar considerations deter the expenditure of capital on the part of the tenant. It must not however be overlooked that under the rack rent system there is no inducement for a tenant to employ his capital in permanent improvements, unless he holds a sufficiently long lease to enable him to secure a satisfactory return on his expenditure.

The custom of Ulster Tenant-right. In some parts of Ireland, especially in Ulster, the amount of rent received by landlords is reduced by what is called the Ulster Tenant-right. According to this custom the incoming tenant pays to the outgoing tenant a certain sum, partly as a consideration for the good will of the farm, and partly as compensation for unexhausted improvements. The sum paid for goodwill is really a part of the economic rent. If the incoming tenant had not to pay this sum, he would be obliged to pay more rent. The custom therefore divides the economic rent into two parts, one of which is capitalized and paid by the incoming tenant to the outgoing tenant; the other part is paid in the usual manner annually to the landlord. The economic advantage of this custom is that it gives practical security of tenure to the tenant, by recognizing that he has a proprietary right in the soil. On the other hand, it is stated that the custom is economically pernicious because it reduces the capital of the incoming tenant just at the time when he wants it most to stock his new farm. In answer to this objection it may be urged that the capital of the tenant would not be invested in the land at all, if it were not for the security of tenure which the tenant-right gives. The practical effect of the Ulster Tenant-right seems to be most satisfactory. Those parts of Ireland where it operates present a most favorable contrast to those districts where no similar custom prevails. The Ulster Custom, although very prevalent, had formerly no legal sanction. Prior to 1870 there were really two laws in Ireland, one the law of the land, and one sanctioned by the customs and habits of the people. The Irish Land Act of 1870 reconciled these two conflicting systems by legalizing the Ulster custom of tenant-right.

The Cottier and Conacre Tenancies of Ireland. The cottier tenancy of Ireland may be described as a tenure in which the rent is forced up beyond the rack rent, by the competition of an excessive population. The nominal rent of a cottier tenure is sometimes fixed at an amount exceeding in value the whole of the produce of the land. Under this wretched system the tenant knows that the landlord would be obliged to leave him just sufficient potatoes to keep himself and his family from starvation. He is never able to pay the full nominal rent; he is therefore constantly in arrears with his landlord. He has no motive for energy and industry, for the landlord would be able to appropriate all the result of his labor in payment of the arrears of rent. At the same time the tenant has no prudential motives to restrain him from marrying and having a numerous family, for he is aware that the landlord could not deprive him and his children of the bare necessaries of life. No system of land tenure can be more mischievous in its economic, social, and moral results than the cottier tenancy of Ireland. This tenure is now much less prevalent than it was before the Irish famine.

There is in Ireland another sort of tenure called conacre. Under this system it was the practice of a landlord who required work done on his estate to pay the laborers by giving them a small plot of manured land rent free.

Having now described the nature of Rent as regulated by competition, and explained the character of some tenures which are controlled by custom, the wages of labor will be next considered.

QUESTIONS ON CHAPTER I. *THE RENT OF LAND*

1. What is rent? Explain what is meant by rents being determined by competition.
2. What is the reason why landlords are able to require a rent for their land?
3. What two elements must always exist in land which pays rent?
4. What determines the rent of any particular land?

5. What is meant by "the margin of cultivation"?
6. What determines the position of the margin of cultivation?
7. Give an illustration of the manner in which the margin of cultivation varies with the price of agricultural produce.
8. What determines the price of agricultural produce?
9. In what two ways is Rent increased by the lowering of the margin of cultivation?
10. Briefly recapitulate Ricardo's theory of Rent.
11. In what sense are the interests of landowners opposed to those of all other classes of the community?
12. In what respects are the interests of landlord, farmer and laborer identical?
13. Show that low wages are not always profitable to the farmer and the landlord.
14. In what way does an increase of population affect the prosperity of a country like Australia?
15. What is the effect of increased population on the prosperity of a country like India?
16. Prove that rent is not a part of the price of agricultural produce.
17. Are rents always regulated by competition?
18. Describe the metayer tenure.
19. Does the landlord under this system get as large a share of the produce as he does where rent is regulated by competition?
20. What are some of the advantages and disadvantages of the metayer tenure?
21. Describe the Ulster Custom of tenant-right. What are its advantages and disadvantages?
22. What is the cottier tenure of Ireland?
23. Describe its disadvantages.
24. What is conacre?
    (a) If a farmer pays a rack rent for his farm, will it make any difference to him whether the land be barren or productive?
    (b) If a hundred square miles of fertile land could be added to the area of England, what effect would it have on the price of agricultural produce?

(c) Would the effect in all probability be permanent?

(d) If you were going to be a farmer, would you rather pay a rack rent, or would you prefer being a metayer tenant?

(e) If all the landlords in England excused their tenants paying rent, would bread be cheaper?

(f) If all farmers instead of paying their rent to private individuals paid it into the national exchequer, what effect would it have on the general wealth of the country?

CHAPTER TWO

The Wages of Labor

That part of wealth which is given in exchange for labor is called wages. In a former chapter it was stated that the portion of circulating capital which was used as the wages of labor was called the wages fund. Hence it was asserted that any circumstance which increases the wages fund tends to raise wages; while an increase in the wages-receiving classes, by adding to the number of those among whom the wages fund is distributed, tends to depress wages.

Wages as regulated by Competition. Wages, like rent, may be regulated either by custom or by competition. They are, however, for the most part, regulated by competition, that is to say, the laborer tries to get as much as possible in exchange for his labor, and the employer tries to obtain labor at the least cost to himself. There are, of course, exceptions to this general assertion; there are many laborers who would not leave an old master in order to gain an increase of wages; and it not unfrequently happens that an employer hires laborers partly out of charity, and would not part with some of his laborers even though he could get their work done for a smaller amount of wages. Such circumstances as these are, however, the exception, and not the rule. Employers and workmen may be regarded as the buyers and sellers of a commodity. Employers want to obtain labor; workmen want to sell it. Employers will try to get labor as cheap as possible, but their competition between themselves tends to raise wages. Suppose that owing to an increase of trade the demand for labor is very active, employers, rather than be deprived of the labor which enables them to obtain their profits, will raise wages in order to retain the services of their employees. The employed try to sell their labor for as much money as possible, but their competition between themselves tends to depress wages. Suppose that three laborers are anxious to obtain work of an employer who only wants the services of one of them. Assuming that all three are equally good workmen, and competition to be unrestricted, the situation will be gained by him who will consent to take the lowest wages. If, on the other hand, three employers are seeking the services of one laborer, he will be hired by the employer who offers the highest wages. It must however be remembered, that the whole industrial population of a country does not compete indiscriminately for all employments. It is rather divided into a series of layers, within each of which considered separately there is a real and effective competition; but as between the different layers or groups competition is practically inoperative. Thus the lowest class of manual laborers are not in competition for the same kind of employment as the skilled artisan; and again, the skilled artisan is not in competition with the professional classes. This limitation of competition is one of the most powerful of the causes which produce different rates of wages in different kinds of employment.

Circumstances which regulate the Amount of Wages. Wages depend on the proportion between the wages fund and the number of the laboring population. If this proportion remains unchanged, the average rate of wages cannot be raised. This should be borne in mind by those who desire to improve the condition of the laborer by raising his wages; for none of these efforts will prove successful if they do not tend either to increase the wages fund or reduce the number of the laboring population. The wages fund increases when a fresh employment for capital is opened, and when, therefore, there is additional inducement to save. The wages fund has been much increased by the introduction of machinery, which by decreasing the cost of production has set free a large quantity of capital and labor, which has been employed by their owners in extending their own trades, or in carrying out new industrial enterprises. In both these cases fresh employment for labor is provided, and the wages fund is increased. Suppose that a manufacturer is carrying on his business with a capital of £10,000, and that he discovers some new process which, by saving time or avoiding waste, reduces the cost of production 10 per-cent. He will now be able to carry on the same business with £9000 which previously required £10,000. There is no reason to suppose that the £1000 which he has saved will be spent unproductively. Even if it is placed in a bank it will be used as capital. But it will in all probability be used by the manufacturer to enlarge his own business. In other words, he will erect new buildings, and employ more labor, fixed and circulating capital are both increased, the wages fund is augmented and wages rise. The wages fund is virtually increased by any circumstance which cheapens food. The wages of labor are in reality increased though no change takes place in the amount of money received by the laborers, if this money will exchange for an increased quantity of bread and meat. A Dorsetshire laborer with 9s. a week was better off when bread was 10d. a gallon, than he was with 10s. a week when bread was 1s. 5d. a gallon.

The influence of Population on Wages. The greatest difficulty in permanently improving the condition of the laboring population arises from the fact that an increase of the wages fund is almost invariably followed by a corresponding increase in the number of the wages-receiving class. At the time of the repeal of the corn laws, it was thought by some ardent repealers that the cheap food which the abolition of the duty on corn brought to every cottage in the kingdom, would permanently improve the condition of the laboring poor; it was said that there would be no more starvation, and no more pauperism. The workhouses, it was confidently asserted, would soon be in ruins. The result has proved far otherwise. The cheap food, which the repeal of the corn laws brought to England, has stimulated a vast increase of population; the benefit which might have been derived from a plentiful supply of cheap food has been absorbed by the demands of millions of hungry mouths. The principal effect, on the laborer, produced by the repeal of the corn laws is that cheap food has enabled him, not to live in greater comfort, but to support an increased number of children. Such considerations lead to the conclusion that no material improvement in the condition of the working classes can be permanent unless it is accompanied by circumstances which will prevent a counterbalancing increase of population.

The importance of raising the Standard of Comfort. No circumstance would prevent overpopulation so effectually as a general raising of the customary standard of comfort among the poorer classes. If they had accustomed themselves to a more comfortable style of living, they would use every effort not again to sink below it. Ricardo says on this subject: "The friends of humanity cannot but wish that in all countries the laboring classes should have a taste for comforts and enjoyments, and that they should be stimulated by all legal means in their exertions to procure them. There cannot be a better security against a superabundant population." It is because there has recently been such a distinct advance in the standard of comfort among the agricultural laborers, that there is every reason to hope that the improvement they have effected in their condition will be permanent. The younger generation are prepared to enter other employments, to move to other localities and emigrate to other countries rather than endure the life which their forefathers led.

Malthus on Population. Malthus, in his celebrated essay on population, showed that there is a constant tendency in animal life to increase beyond the nourishment prepared for it, and that therefore unless there are some checks placed upon population the total production of food would in course of time be insufficient to supply the wants of mankind. It has been thought by some that Malthus was manifestly in the wrong, because there appears no likelihood of the means of subsistence becoming insufficient for the wants of the population of the globe. It must, however, be remembered that what Malthus said was, that this insufficiency would prevail if there were no checks on population. These checks do exist, and are in active operation in every country; that is to say, in every country either the total number of births of which the population is capable does not take place, or else a large proportion of those who are born, die. The population is kept down, either by prudence, or by such agencies as war, famine, and pestilence. The germs of existence both in the animal and vegetable kingdoms, if they could freely develop themselves, would, as Malthus showed, fill millions of worlds in the course of a few thousand years. "Necessity, that imperious, all-pervading law of nature, restrains them within the prescribed limits. . . . In plants and irrational animals the view of the subject is simple. . . . Wherever there is liberty, the power of increase is exerted; and the superabundant effects are repressed afterwards by want of room and nourishment." He then showed that man had the same tendency to increase beyond his means of subsistence, and that where no other checks restrained the increase of population it is reduced by the difficulty of obtaining food, by disease, and by other agencies which bring misery and degradation in their train. But beside these positive checks on population, there are also preventive or prudential checks; and in his essay on population he examines the condition of many countries in order to ascertain whether the prudential or the positive check is the more operative. In most countries both checks are in operation: in London the number of children who die of diseases produced by want of food, clothing and attention, and from overcrowding, is appalling, and is a blot upon the civilization of this country; for it is hardly necessary to say that as civilization advances, the prudential check grows stronger, and the positive check less active. The civilization of a country might also be measured by comparing the activity of the prudential check with that of the positive check.

A right conception of the importance of population is fundamental to an understanding of the causes which regulate the wages of labor. An increase in population, unaccompanied by counterbalancing circumstances, acts upon the condition of the laborer in two ways; it increases the price of food by rendering a resort to less productive soils necessary; and by increasing the number of the wages-receiving class it decreases the share which each receives from the wages fund.

Emigration is an insufficient remedy for Overpopulation. Emigration has been considered by some a sufficient remedy for overpopulation. There are, however, many objections to relying on emigration as the sole means of checking the natural increase of population. In the first place, those who are the poorest and the most destitute have not the means to emigrate, and if means were provided by the government or by a national subscription, the colonies would very probably object to being made the receptacles of the pauperism of the Old World. Those that we are anxious to get rid of the colonies would not accept; and those who are prosperous and in good employment would have no motive to leave their occupations. In the second place, unless prudential checks are in operation, the place of those who have emigrated will soon be filled by a new generation. And, in the third place, emigration cannot be looked upon as a permanent remedy for overpopulation, because in the course of time the colonies will be as thickly peopled as the old countries of Europe now are, and the principal advantage of emigration will then cease to exist. Notwithstanding the incompleteness of this remedy for overpopulation, emigration may at the present time do great good, if it is accompanied by increased activity of the preventive or prudential check upon population. For some time to come every skilled laborer who reaches America or Australia will be a source of wealth to those nations, while his absence will tend to reduce the overstocked labor markets of Europe. The emigration of laborers from Ireland to America has no doubt been very serviceable to both countries; and a somewhat similar movement on the part of English agricultural laborers, although on a very much smaller scale, has recently produced a very marked improvement on the condition of those who have remained at home, while skilled farmhands are most warmly welcomed in Canada, the United States, and New Zealand.

The effect on Wages of a Local Decline in Profits. A historical survey shows that the rate of profit has in all countries declined with the increase of wealth and population. The causes which have produced this universal decline in the rate of profit will be investigated in the next chapter; it is sufficient here to show the influence on wages of a local and not a general decline of profits. Suppose that the laborers engaged in any particular trade are receiving such an amount of wages that their employer's capital is remunerated by no more than the average rate of profit. If these men strike for higher wages, and succeed in obtaining them, the employer will carry on his business at a comparative loss, that is, he will be receiving less profit than he would realize in other trades. He will therefore be careful not to extend his business; and if the loss remain permanent he will gradually withdraw his capital, and invest it in other trades. The benefit, therefore, that the laborers derive from a rise in wages which causes profits to sink below the average rate, is only temporary. If it be true that previous to the agricultural strikes which have lately taken place, farmers were gaining something less than the ordinary rate of profit upon their capital, the success of the laborers in obtaining higher wages must produce a change in the conditions of agricultural industry. The farmers will not go on employing their capital for a less reward than they could obtain in other employments. Possibly the increased wages will make labor more efficient; if this be the case, the farmer will be compensated for his extra outlay by better crops, or by employing fewer hands. Possibly the higher rate of wages will induce the farmer to use more machinery than he has hitherto done; the size of farms will be increased, and the use of the steam plow, the reaping machine, and the haymaking machine will become universal. If this be the case, the farmer will employ comparatively few men; and those he does employ will be highly skilled agricultural mechanics who will receive correspondingly high wages. In the meantime the extinction or the removal of the old-fashioned laborer, of the type suggested by the nickname "Hodge," will be a process accompanied by acute suffering and much bitter heartburning. Hodge is not quick to emigrate, he is still less quick in developing into an agricultural engineer, or a town artisan; and his sufferings must be put down as a setoff against the advantages of a highly skilled and highly paid class of agricultural laborers. There is another way in which the farmer may be compensated for his loss, if his profits are reduced below the ordinary rate in consequence of the higher wages obtained by the laborers. His rent may be reduced. If this alternative be practicable, it would be accompanied by far less suffering than that involved in the summary extinction of Hodge.

The Effect of increased Efficiency upon the rate of Wages. Another means of increasing the wages fund is provided by any circumstance which increases the efficiency of labor. If more wealth is produced by the joint agency of land, labor, and capital, there will be more to distribute as rent to the landlord, wages to the laborer, and profits to the capitalist. If education, or any similar agency, should cause the laborer to work with more intelligence and with more honesty, the efficiency of labor would be increased. The laborer would make a better use of his tools and materials, and the labor of superintendence and watching might be dispensed with; in this way the wages fund might be increased, because more wealth would be produced; the cost of production at the same time would be diminished and the salary of the overlooker would be saved. Hitherto, as previously explained, circumstances, such as the repeal of the corn laws, which ought to have produced an improvement in the condition of the poor, have exerted little permanent effect in this direction, because the additional wealth which was temporarily enjoyed encouraged earlier and more improvident marriages, and thus an increase of population was stimulated. The wages fund has indeed been vastly increased, but the number of the wages-receiving classes has increased with corresponding rapidity. The physical condition of the poor must therefore be improved by other than material agencies. Habits of prudence and foresight, accompanied by the adoption of a higher standard of comfort, can alone produce a permanent effect in ameliorating the condition of the poorest class of laborers.

Local and temporary circumstances cause the Rate of Wages constantly to fluctuate. The above remarks indicate the general causes which regulate the wages of labor, but it must not be overlooked that local and temporary circumstances produce great fluctuations in the rate of wages. Just as the price of commodities continually varies on each side of the sum which is exactly sufficient to provide the current rate of wages and profits to their producers, so the price of particular kinds of labor constantly fluctuates above and below the general average, produced by the proportion between the wages fund and the number of the laboring population.

Do High Prices produce High wages? It is sometimes said that high prices produce high wages. The meaning of such an expression will be rightly understood only by those who know that no circumstance can produce a permanent effect upon the condition of the laboring population, if the ratio between the wages fund and the number of the wages-receiving classes remains unchanged. Bearing this fact in mind, let us investigate some instances in which it is said that high prices produce high wages, and that low prices produce low wages. There are many cases in which high prices produce no effect whatever upon wages. Prices of articles the supply of which can be increased depend upon cost of production. Cost of production consists of the following elements: labor, abstinence and risk. No one will incur either of these elements of cost without receiving as great a reward as he can obtain; the price of the article must therefore provide the current rate of wages and profits. If an increased amount of labor, abstinence and risk is required to produce the commodity, its price must be increased; or if any circumstance should enable its producers to secure a larger reward for their services, its price must also be increased. In the first case where we supposed that a greater exertion of labor, abstinence, and risk was necessary to produce the commodity, its price would necessarily be increased without raising either the profits of capital or the wages of labor. The price of an article may also be increased by taxation, without any corresponding increase in the wages of labor. There are however some circumstances in which increased prices produce a temporary effect in raising wages. Suppose that there is a greatly increased demand for such a commodity as cotton cloth. For a time the equalization between demand and supply will be effected by increasing the price of cotton goods. The new prices will perhaps provide the manufacturers with exceptionally large profits, and this circumstance will cause a largely increased supply of cotton goods. For this purpose the employment of new capital will be required, the manufacturers will perhaps erect new mills, and employ new capital in setting up machinery; to work this machinery an increased number of laborers will be required. This increased demand for labor will cause an increase in wages; here, then, is a case in which high prices have produced high wages. But these high prices and high wages are sure to attract the competition of other manufacturers and other laborers, who think that they would like to share these high profits and high wages. Production is therefore still further augmented in consequence of the competition of other capitalists; the supply of labor is also largely increased owing to the competition of other laborers. The increase of the supply causes the price of cotton cloth to return to a point closely approximating to its former position; the price may even sink below what is necessary to provide the ordinary rate of wages and profits current in the trade before the rise took place. In either of these cases wages and profits must both decline in a degree corresponding with the fall in price. The manner in which the fall of wages is brought about may be described as follows: production is checked; manufacturers no longer realize exceptionally high profits; they may perhaps be making less than the ordinary rate of profit. Hence they will strive to reduce the supply; they will not extend their buildings, and they may probably keep their men on at half-time. In such a case what will be the effect on the wages of labor? We have supposed that the high wages which accompanied the original increased supply, attracted a large number of workmen, who were anxious to share the prosperity of the trade. Hence when trade is dull and manufacturers are desirous of reducing production, there is a largely increased number of workmen who are seeking employment. These circumstances must undoubtedly produce a decline in wages. If the men resist such a decrease and refuse to work for lower wages, it might be to the manufacturer's interest, if his profits were less than the ordinary rate, to shut up his mills; and in this event thousands of workmen would be out of employment altogether. In thus illustrating the temporary nature of the effect of high prices upon wages, an extreme case has perhaps been taken. In all cases, however, where the competition between laborers is active, exceptionally high wages are sure to produce an additional supply of labor, which will, sooner or later, reduce wages to their former level. This is an illustration of the theory of supply and demand, as explained in a previous section. When the demand for labor is in excess of the supply, an equalization between demand and supply is effected by an increase in the price of labor. The higher wages, however, attract an increased supply of labor, and the equalization finally takes place at a lower rate of wages. An illustration of the effect of high prices on wages may be taken from the recent great rise in the price of coal and the subsequent additions made to the wages of the miners. In this case the miners were able to obtain the maximum of advantage; they were really masters of the situation because they possessed what almost amounted to a natural monopoly of the trade. Other laborers unused to the work could not be introduced to compete with them and run down wages; as they possessed this advantage, they were able for some time to prevent the price of coal from going down by strictly limiting the supply, or, as it is called, the "output" of each man per week. Hence they made the most of their opportunities.

Where competition is active the effect of a local depression of Trade upon Wages is only temporary. When wages are below the average and trade is dull, an influence is exerted by these very circumstances to restore wages and profits to their normal condition. Manufacturers will not go on producing commodities at a comparative loss, and intelligent workmen will not go on laboring at an occupation in which they receive lower wages than they could obtain elsewhere. The supply of capital and labor engaged in the depressed trade is accordingly reduced; production is decreased, and the supply being diminished prices rise, and wages are restored to their former level.

Charitable donations often interfere mischievously with the operation of Competition. It frequently happens that when an industry is much depressed, and the profits and wages realized in it are very small, there is temporarily great distress among the workmen, numbers of whom are thrown out of work altogether. Where competition is active, and no efforts are made to check its operation, many of the workmen will, under such circumstances, find work in other employments, and frequently in other localities; the distress in this way is relieved without the agency of private charity or parochial assistance. In too many instances, however, workmen are encouraged, by the help they receive from the poor rates and private charity, to remain in the locality where trade is depressed, and not to seek fresh employment elsewhere. A striking instance of this well-meant but mischievous interference was exhibited in the Lancashire cotton famine. During the American war the supply of raw cotton, which had hitherto been obtained from the southern states of the Union, almost entirely ceased. The manufacture of cotton cloth is the staple industry of Lancashire, many thousands of artisans being engaged in it. The civil war in America, by checking the supply of the raw material, completely paralyzed the cotton trade of Lancashire. Manufacturers suffered heavy losses, and thousands of workmen were out of employment. The suddenness and severity of the misfortunes of the poor people who were thus on the brink of starvation appealed powerfully to the sympathies of the whole country. Subscriptions were set on foot in the remotest parts of the kingdom. Relieving societies were formed who were in weekly receipt of large sums of money, which they devoted to the support of the cotton operatives and their families. The workmen, therefore, instead of migrating to Belfast, Dundee, Bradford, and other towns, in which the linen and woolen trades were at the same time exceptionally active, were induced to stay in Lancashire, in consequence of the charity which was so liberally dispensed to them. It is a fact that during the distress in Lancashire the total manufacture of textile fabrics did not diminish; for the falling off in the supply of cotton caused a greatly increased production of linen and woolen goods. Had the Lancashire operatives migrated to those localities, where their labor would have been welcomed, the distress would have been alleviated, and the depression in the cotton trade would not have lasted so long. It was many years before Lancashire recovered from the ill effects of the charity which she received during the cotton famine. A large part of her population was permanently pauperized; and for years after the cessation of the war a great number of the mills were worked only on half time, because the number of operatives was so much greater than the production required.

Such an instance as this is a most striking example of the harm that may be done by interfering with the operation of competition. Had those who organized the relieving societies during the Lancashire famine remembered that competition tends to make the effect of good or bad trade upon wages only temporary, they would have hesitated before they used such powerful means to check the operation of competition. Had it even been recognized that the free migration of labor from one locality to another was the best means of preventing permanent distress among laborers, the kindly intentions of the charitable might have been satisfied by using some part of their subscriptions to assist the cotton operatives to migrate to those localities where their labor was so urgently required. It is frequently said that the best means of helping the poor is to help them to help themselves. If this principle were acted upon as often as it is asserted, the effects of charity would be less disastrous.

Although it is possible to make unfavorable criticisms on the manner in which national charity was dispensed during the cotton famine, it should never be forgotten that the Lancashire operatives behaved most nobly throughout the whole period of their distress; it was worth something that cannot be measured in money, that the whole country testified its sympathy with their misfortunes, and its admiration for the heroic courage with which those misfortunes were borne.

Free competition among laborers always tends to reduce exceptionally high wages, and to raise wages when they are exceptionally low. Competition, however, acts much more slowly in equalizing the price of labor in different localities than in regulating the price of commodities. The difference between the price of corn, for instance, in London and in the most remote counties in England, can never remain in excess of the cost of conveying the corn from the one place to the other. The price of labor is, however, not so readily influenced by competition. A laborer may be aware that he will earn 2s. a week more by migrating to an adjoining county, but he has to consider whether he has the means of meeting the expense of removing himself, his family, and his little stock of furniture. He may also be reluctant to forsake the place in which he has spent all his life, and to leave his old friends.

Competition is almost inoperative among the Agricultural Laborers. Such feelings as these have until very recently acted very powerfully with the agricultural laborers. Many of them were very simple ignorant people, who had never been beyond the limits of their own parishes. To them a place a hundred miles off was more unknown, and apparently more inaccessible, than Central Africa is to an ordinarily well-informed person. Hence competition, which must always act more slowly on the price of labor than on that of commodities, was almost inoperative in many agricultural districts. As previously explained, this state of things is gradually coming to an end. Cheap railways and the penny post have brought all the places in such a country as England close together, and agricultural laborers are beginning to move from places where wages are low to places where wages are higher, almost as freely as the ordinary artisan.

The strikes that have lately occurred among agricultural laborers in different parts of the country have, among other effects, caused a considerable amount of migration and emigration to take place. There can be little doubt that the movement for higher wages will gradually spread all over the country, and that migration and emigration will follow as the natural consequences of the peasant waking up to the fact that it is possible for him to better his condition.

Adam Smith's Five Causes which produce Differences of Wages in different employments. If competition acted freely among all classes of laborers, the inequalities of wages for the same work in different localities would cease to exist. There are, however, differences in wages in different employments which are permanent in their character. Adam Smith has thus enumerated the five causes which produce different rates of wages in various employments:

First. The agreeableness or disagreeableness of the employments themselves.

Second. The easiness and cheapness, or the difficulty and expense, of learning them.

Third. The constancy or inconstancy of employment in them.

Fourth. The small or great trust which must be reposed in those who exercise them.

Fifth. The probability or improbability of success in them.

To these must be added the limitation of competition among the higher and lower sections or groups into which laborers are divided, and which practically limits the choice of a laborer, selecting his employment, to trades of about the same grade as that in which he was born. The son of an agricultural laborer, for instance, would be as powerless to choose the employment of a banker's clerk as he would be to select that of a prime minister or an archbishop.

Mining industry affords several examples of the manner in which the agreeableness or disagreeableness of an employment acts upon the wages of those engaged in it. The miners who work underground receive much higher wages than those who are employed in the less dangerous and more agreeable occupation of breaking, sifting, and washing the ore on the surface. No workmen would enter into an occupation which is exceptionally dangerous or injurious to the health, unless they were compensated for the risk they incur by an exceptionally high rate of wages. Those who labor in a coal mine receive, over and above the ordinary wages current in the district, a sum sufficient to induce them to risk their lives in a peculiarly dangerous occupation. Other things being equal, the more dangerous a mine is, the higher are the wages of those engaged in working it.

Under the head "agreeableness or disagreeableness of an employment" may be included those occupations which bring respect or contempt and dislike upon those who practice them. The payment given in exchange for the services of officers in the army and clergymen is, as a rule, extremely small. Many, however, enter the church or the army on account of the social position which members of these professions obtain. The dignity accruing to their position is a compensation for the small remuneration which they receive. On the other hand, those who practice a trade which brings upon its members contempt and dislike are compensated by a large amount of wages. No one would voluntarily undertake the duties of a hangman, for example, if he were not induced to do so by the hope of receiving exceptionally large wages. It is not an uncommon circumstance for a nobleman to give his cook a higher salary than his private secretary. This may be partly accounted for by the fact that a certain amount of contempt attaches to the office of a man cook, whereas the employment of a secretary is considered to be quite compatible with the character and position of an educated gentleman.

It is also obvious that the higher salary earned by the cook is in great part due to the second of Adam Smith's causes. If wages in any employment are influenced by the easiness and cheapness, or the difficulty and expense of learning it, it is not unreasonable that the cook should have more wages than the secretary. Any moderately well educated person is capable of performing the duties of a secretary at a day's notice: whereas a really first-rate cook cannot perhaps be made in less than five years, and he will probably remain a student of culinary art all his life. Compare the work of a man like Soyer with the ordinary routine work of a secretary, and it is obvious that the capacity to perform the first is difficult and expensive to acquire, while it is the easiest and least expensive thing in the world for a man of ordinary education to acquire a complete knowledge of the second.

There are many industries which require a long apprenticeship before skill in them can be secured; and there are other industrial operations which can be almost as well performed by a novice as by a practiced hand. These differences produce a corresponding difference in the rates of wages. A shipwright or a glassblower has to spend many years in acquiring the skill which his trade requires. During the first half of a long apprenticeship, he earns nothing at all; considerable expense is therefore incurred by him in learning his trade. For this expense, and for the difficulties which have to be overcome in acquiring the necessary skill, he will in afterlife be compensated by receiving a higher rate of wages than those workmen whose occupation entails neither difficulty nor expense. The trade of a crossing sweeper, for instance, and that of a copying clerk are very easy and cheap to acquire. A broom is all that is required in the one case, and a knowledge of reading and writing in the other. Hence wages in such employments are much smaller than those earned by the skilled mechanic.

Difficulty of attainment is a most important element in determining wages in those employments where the requisite skill is acquired partly by long practice and is partly the result of natural endowments. The large remuneration received by first-class opera singers, for example, is not due solely to the expense of acquiring their proficiency. An inferior singer may have taken quite as much pains to cultivate her voice, and may also have incurred as great an expense in obtaining her musical education. The reason why *prime donne* obtain such large sums is that they possess what may be described as a natural monopoly. There is a very general demand for the best kind of vocal music, which few beside themselves can give. The same remark applies to some of the highest kinds of manual labor, such, for instance, as are required in the more delicate operations of watchmaking.

The constancy or inconstancy of an employment produces an influence on the rate of wages prevailing in it. No one would enter an employment in which on an average he would only be able to work nine months in the year, if he were not compensated by receiving during these nine months an exceptionally high rate of wages. Some trades, such as malting, cannot be carried on in hot weather; others, such as building, are stopped by frost; dockyard laborers are liable to perpetual interruptions in their employment. Such workmen, therefore, as maltsters, bricklayers, and dockyard laborers, receive a higher rate of wages than they would be able to obtain if they were not liable to be frequently out of work.

The amount of trust which must be reposed in those engaged in a particular occupation exercises a very great influence upon the wages they receive. The more trustworthiness required the higher must be the wages given. It is essential that such persons as bankers, cashiers, jewelers' assistants, engine drivers, railway guards, policemen, and postmen, should be men in whom a considerable amount of confidence can with safety be reposed. Men are not placed in these positions until they have shown their employers that the uprightness and steadiness of their characters can be relied on. When they have proved themselves to be trustworthy they can justly claim a higher rate of wages as a compensation for the responsibility which their position entails.

In most trades the prospect of success is almost a certainty; an agricultural laborer or a journeyman tailor cannot have many doubts as to the probability of his succeeding in the trade he has chosen. Such considerations as these apply more to the professions than to trades; but there are some cases in which wages are influenced by the probability or improbability of success. A man who is about to emigrate may well feel that there is considerable uncertainty whether he will succeed in the new life upon which he is about to enter. He may not know whether he will find work in the colony to which he proposes to go; but he is certain that if he does get work he will receive higher wages than he could ever hope to earn at home.

The fact that different rates of wages prevail in different employments does not in the least invalidate the principle previously laid down; viz. that wages depend on the ratio between the wages fund and the number of the laboring population. If a cake is going to be divided between a party of children, it is perfectly correct to say that the quantity of cake which each will receive depends on the ratio between the size of the cake and the number of the children. It does not follow that each child will receive an equal share; but the *average* size of each share can be correctly ascertained by those who know the number of the children and the size of the cake. If there are twenty-four children and the cake weighs 1½ lb., the average weight of each child's share will be one ounce. One child may receive more and another less, but while the number of the children and the size of the cake remain the same, the average size of the shares is unalterable. In the same way, while the wages fund and the number of the laboring population remain the same, the average rate of wages cannot be affected; if one set of laborers receives more, another must be receiving less.

QUESTIONS ON CHAPTER II. *THE WAGES OF LABOR*

1. What are wages? Is custom or competition the main regulator of wages?
2. How is the average rate of wages determined?
3. In what manner alone, therefore, can the condition of the laboring classes be improved?
4. By what means has the wages fund, in such a country as this, been greatly increased?
5. Why has not the condition of the laborer improved in proportion to this increase of the wages fund?
6. Describe the principal effect of the repeal of the corn laws upon the condition of the laborer.
7. What are the main features of Malthus' essay on population?
8. Into what classes does he divide the checks upon population?
9. As civilization advances, which of these checks becomes the more powerful?
10. In what two ways does an increase of population deteriorate the condition of the laborer?
11. Why is emigration an insufficient remedy for overpopulation?
12. Describe the influence of the average rate of profit upon the wages fund.
13. Are laborers ultimately benefited by an increase of wages which reduces their employers' profits below the average rate?
14. How does the increased efficiency of labor affect the wages fund?
15. Is the price of labor subject to fluctuations?
16. Do high prices produce high wages? Give illustrations.
17. Describe the manner in which competition raises exceptionally low wages, and reduces exceptionally high wages.
18. Show by an example that harm is done by inducing laborers to remain in a locality where trade is exceptionally depressed.
19. Why does competition act much more slowly upon the wages of labor than upon the prices of commodities?
20. Indicate some of the limitations of competition as between different classes of laborers.
21. Among what class of laborers is competition almost inoperative?

22. Enumerate Adam Smith's five causes which produce different rates of wages in different employments.

23. Give examples of the effect of these five causes upon wages.

24. Show by an illustration that the fact of different rates of wages prevailing in different employments, does not affect the truth of the proposition that the average rate of wages depends upon the ratio between the wages fund and the number of the laboring population.

(a) An article on the Census in the *Daily News* in July 1871, began thus: "The preliminary report of the Registrar General on the population of England and Wales, as shown by the Census of this year, is a splendid monument of the growth and prosperity of the country. The population has increased beyond expectation. There were 2,637,884 persons living in England and Wales last April more than there were ten years before. This increase is the largest ever made in any ten years of English history." Write a criticism on these sentences, bearing in mind that in London within the period referred to the cost of outdoor pauperism increased 130 percent; and that in England and Wales, between the years 1866 and 1869, indoor pauperism increased 17 percent, and outdoor pauperism 10½ percent.

(b) Will the laborers in a depressed trade be more benefited by receiving charity or by being assisted to migrate to other localities where their labor is required?

(c) In November 1870, this paragraph appeared in a daily paper. "The population engaged in the production of coal and iron are recovering from depression, and are again marrying and giving in marriage at their usual pace." What effect will this have on the prosperity of the workmen in the iron and coal trades?

(d) Is the fact that one blackbird can do very well in a cage, any reason for supposing that twenty blackbirds in the same cage would do equally well?

(e) Give any reasons which are suggested by the contents of the last chapter, why the salaries earned by governesses are in general so small compared with those which are earned by men engaged in teaching.

ON THE PROFITS OF CAPITAL

PROFIT IS THE REWARD OF CAPITAL FOR THE SERVICE IT RENDERS in the Production of Wealth. Capital was defined, in a previous Section, as that part of wealth which is set aside to assist future production. Capital is consequently the result of saving; but, in order to fulfill its functions, it must be either wholly or partially consumed. It is now evident that the owners of wealth will not consent to its being appropriated to assist future production, unless they are rewarded by a share of the produce. This share is termed profits. It is thought by some, that it is an injustice that capital should receive any reward for its part in the production of wealth. Capitalists are by such persons denounced as selfish usurers, and the interest which their wealth returns to them is regarded as if it had been stolen from the public. M. Bastiat combated these notions (which at one time were very prevalent in France) in a series of little tracts, in which by a number of examples he showed the real nature of the profits of capital, "proving that it is lawful, and explaining why it should be perpetual." The following is an abridgement of one of his examples.

There was once in a village a poor carpenter, who worked hard from morning to night. One day James thought to himself, "With my hatchet, saw, and hammer, I can only make coarse furniture, and can only get the pay for such. If I had a plane I should please my customers more, and they would pay me more. Yes, I am resolved, I will make myself a plane." At the end of ten days, James had in his possession an admirable plane, which he valued all the more for having made it himself. While he was reckoning all the profits which he expected to derive from the use of it, he was interrupted by William, a carpenter in the neighboring village. William, having admired the plane, was struck with the advantages which might be gained from it. He said to James:

"You must do me a service; lend me the plane for a year." As might be expected James cried out, "How can you think of such a thing, William? Well, if I do you this service, what will you do for me in return?"

W. Nothing. Don't you know that a loan ought to be gratuitous?

J. I know nothing of the sort; but I do know that if I were to lend you my plane for a year, it would be giving it to you. To tell you the truth, that was not what I made it for.

W. Very well, then; I ask you to do me a service; what service do you ask me in return?

J. First, then, in a year the plane will be done for. You must therefore give me another exactly like it.

W. That is perfectly just. I submit to these conditions. I think you must be satisfied with this and can require nothing further.

J. I think otherwise. I made the plane for myself and not for you. I expected to gain some advantage from it. I have made the plane for the purpose of improving my work and my condition; if you merely return it to me in a year, it is you who will gain the profit of it during the whole of that time. I am not bound to do you such a service without receiving anything in return. Therefore, if you wish for my plane, besides the restoration already bargained for, you must give me a new plank as a compensation for the advantages of which I shall be deprived.

These terms were agreed to, but the singular part of it is that at the end of the year, when the plane came into James' possession, he lent it again; recovered it, and lent it a third and fourth time. It has passed into the hands of his son, who still lends it. Let us examine this little story. The plane is the symbol of all capital, and the plank is the symbol of all interest. If therefore the yielding of the plank by the borrower to the lender is a natural and equitable remuneration, we may conclude that it is natural and equitable that capital should produce interest. We may also conclude that interest is not injurious to the borrower. James and William are perfectly free as regards the transaction to which the plane gave rise. The fact of William consenting to borrow proves that he considers it an advantage to himself. He borrows, because he gains by borrowing.

The Profits of Capital are composed of three elements. The interest on capital, namely the sum which a borrower gives to the lender for the consideration of a loan, forms only a part of the Profits of Capital. The Profits of Capital are composed of three elements: interest on capital, compensation for risk, and wages of superintendence. The interest on capital, at any particular time and in any country, can be ascertained by the interest yielded, at the same time and in the same country, by those securities which involve no risk and no labor of superintendence. In this country, Government stock affords such a security. Those who invest money in the funds are with reason confident that they run no risk of losing it, and the possession of stock does not involve any labor. The owners of Government stock receive about $3\frac{1}{4}$ percent interest on their capital, and therefore $3\frac{1}{4}$ percent is the current rate of interest at the present time in this country. If more than this is now given in this country for a loan, it is because the lender has not complete confidence in the ability of the borrower to pay; and therefore compensation for risk increases the sum which is given for the loan. If the profits of capital were no greater than the interest on capital, no one would take the trouble or incur the risk of entering into business. If the employment of money in trade yielded only a profit of 3¼ percent, merchants and shopkeepers would withdraw their capital from business and buy Government securities. The profits of capital are greatest in those pursuits in which the greatest risk is incurred and where the labor of superintendence is most costly; the variableness of these two elements produces great variations in the rate of profit in different trades. A butcher, for instance, realizes larger profits than a draper because his labor of superintendence is more disagreeable, and he also incurs greater risk, for in this climate a thunderstorm or a sudden alteration from cool weather to intense heat is often sufficient to destroy his whole stock of meat.

In uncivilized countries, the insecurity of property causes compensation for risk to form a very large proportion of the profits of capital. Speaking of the state of society in some parts of Asia, Mr. Mill says, "Those who lend, under these wretched governments, do so at the utmost peril of never being paid. In most of the native states of India, the lowest terms on which anyone will lend money, even to the government, are such that if the interest is paid only for a few years, and the principal not at all, the lender is tolerably well indemnified." It is notorious that a spendthrift who has run through all his own property, can raise money only by promising an enormously high rate of interest. The moneylenders exact from him 60 or 70 percent as interest, for they know that there is a very great chance that they will never be paid at all. If they are paid, their profits are sufficiently large to compensate them for their frequent losses. There was a case in the papers a short time since of a Cambridge undergraduate who borrowed money at the rate of 75 percent. The father of the young man refused to pay the debt because his son was not of age when it was contracted, and the law upheld him in his refusal. But the moneylender can well afford occasionally to lose both principal and interest, because it appears that he is able to find a considerable number of young men foolish enough to accept loans from him on the exorbitant terms just quoted. The profits of the moneylender are increased not merely by his risk of loss, but by the dishonorable character of his business, which protects him from the competition of honest men, and from that of men who, whether they are honest or the reverse, desire the good opinion and esteem of their neighbors.

The Rate of Interest is the same in all trades in the same country and at the same time. If compensation for risk and for dishonorable reputation, together with the wages of superintendence, are eliminated from profits, the interest on capital alone remaining, the amount of this interest will remain constant in all trades at the same time and in the same country. The interest on the capital of the farmer, the grocer, and the manufacturer inevitably tends to an equality, at the same time and in the same place; the differences in the *profits* of these individuals are caused by the differences in the risk and reputation which they incur and in the wages which they receive for superintendence. It is not therefore true that profits in different trades tend to an equality; for the risk in some occupations is permanently greater than in others, and this risk must receive compensation; some trades also require more superintendence than others; and the wages paid for particular kinds of labor vary in the manner described in the previous chapter. There must therefore always be natural and permanent differences in the rate of profit in different employments. The interest on capital alone remains constant in various trades at the same time and in the same country.

An explanation of the causes which produce a decline in the Rate of Interest as Wealth and Population increase. An inquiry may now be made into the causes which produce a decline in the rate of interest, as wealth and population increase. This leads to a very interesting example of Ricardo's theory of Rent. The amount of the reward given to labor and capital must ultimately depend on their efficiency. That is to say, any circumstance which causes the same amount of labor and capital to produce more wealth must, if other things remain unchanged, produce a corresponding increase in wages and interest. On the other hand, any circumstance which causes a given quantity of labor and capital to produce less wealth diminishes the amount distributed as wages and interest. If while a man is consuming a sack of wheat he can produce a sack and a half, the reward for his labor and capital is at the rate of 50 percent. But if he has to move away to less fertile land so that he only produces a sack and a quarter of wheat, while he consumes a sack, his wages and profits are reduced to 25 percent. As the margin of cultivation descends, that is to say, as land of less and less fertility has to be cultivated to supply the needs of the population, wages and profits tend to decline, and rents to increase; because rent is the excess in productiveness of any particular land, over the worst land in cultivation that pays no rent. Ricardo's theory shows that, as population increases, the augmented demand for food causes a resort to less fertile or less conveniently situated soils. The required food is therefore produced at a greater proportionate expenditure of capital and labor; in other words, a given amount of labor and capital is less productive of wealth, and wages and interest consequently decline.

The Law of Diminishing Productiveness. A similar effect is produced if the additional food required has to be raised upon land already in cultivation. When agriculture has advanced to a certain stage, in the absence of any special discoveries doubling the capital and labor applied to any particular land does not double the produce; "or to express the same thing in other words every increase of produce is obtained by a more than proportional increase in the application of labor to the land." J. S. Mill, *Principles of Pol. E.* Vol I. p. 217. Every successive *dose* of capital applied to the land yields a less and less return. If it were otherwise, if every *dose* of capital yielded a proportional return, the whole economic condition of the world would be changed. A single farm might raise produce sufficient for a whole nation; and the only limit to the increase of population would be that of finding standing room.

The law of diminishing productiveness shows why profits and wages tend to decline, and why they are much higher in a new than in an old country.

The following illustration will suffice to prove that, in fact, this is the case. In England wages and interest are much lower than they are in Australia. In England the margin of cultivation is very low: soils are here cultivated, with the greatest care, which would not be used at all in Australia. The same amount of capital and labor, expended in agriculture, is much more productive of wealth in Australia than in England; hence the reward of labor and capital is greater in the former country than in the latter. From these facts it is proved that profits do not depend upon the wages of labor, but upon the efficiency of labor; that is to say, upon the proportion which the amount of wages paid bears to the productiveness of labor. In Australia wages are much higher than in England, but the cost of labor is less because labor is much more productive in Australia than in England. That this is true is proved by the fact that profits are much greater in Australia than in England, and the rate of interest is also higher.

High prices do not denote large profits. Nothing can be more erroneous than to suppose that high prices invariably denote large profits. It is true that a sudden demand for a commodity sometimes causes its price to be temporarily raised beyond what is sufficient to return the ordinary rate of profits and wages to its producers. But, as frequently explained, the competition of capital and labor causes these high wages and profits to be reduced; prices being permanently regulated, where free competition prevails, by cost of production. In the previous chapter it was explained that high prices do not produce high wages; the same reasoning applies to the case now before us. Take as an example the price of cotton goods. The cost of production consists of the following elements: labor, abstinence and risk; the cost of an article may also be increased by taxation. An increase in any of these elements will increase the cost of production, and consequently tend to raise the price of commodities. For instance the labor necessary to the production of the cotton may be greatly increased, owing to the sudden failure of the ordinary sources of supply; or increased taxation may be imposed on the raw material or on the manufactured cotton; in either of these cases prices will be augmented without causing any increase in the profits of capital; in fact the increased cost of all the other elements of cost of production would actually tend to diminish the profits of capital; and therefore higher prices would be accompanied by a decline in the rate of profit. At the time of the American war, the difficulty and expense of obtaining raw cotton very greatly increased the price of cotton goods; at the same time manufacturers were sustaining heavy losses, and wages were so much reduced that the memorable cotton famine ensued. That high prices do not make high profits is shown by the simple consideration that the rate of profit represents a proportion, and that a proportion cannot be determined by one factor simply, but depends on the relation in which this stands to the other. The rate of interest in fact depends on the costliness of the other elements of cost of production, and as by far the most important of these elements is labor, it is sufficiently accurate to say, as stated above, that the rate of interest depends on the cost of labor. It has frequently been stated that both profits and wages must ultimately be contained in the price realized by the article produced by the joint exertion of capital and labor. Hence it is seen that the greater the proportion of this price which has to be conceded to labor, in the form of wages, the less remains to be enjoyed by the capitalist, as profits. Cost of Labor *to the Capitalist,* therefore, depends on the proportion of the value of the product, due to the joint exertions of capital and labor, which is secured as the reward of labor.

On what does the Cost of labor depend? It is now therefore desirable to ascertain accurately on what the cost of labor to the capitalist depends. Mr. Mill has described the cost of labor as a "function of three variables." That is to say, the cost of labor to the capitalist is influenced by three circumstances, each of which is liable to variations.

These circumstances are

1. "The efficiency of labor.
2. The wages of labor (meaning thereby the real reward of the laborer).
3. The greater or less cost at which the articles composing that real reward can be produced or purchased."

If the efficiency of labor is increased while the wages of labor and the cost of the necessaries of life are unaltered, the cost of labor to the capitalist is diminished. If the wages of labor are increased, without a corresponding increase in the efficiency of labor, the cost of labor to the capitalist is increased.

If the articles composing the real reward of the laborer become less costly, without his obtaining more of them, wages decline and the cost of labor, to the capitalist, is diminished.

The rate of profit depends upon the share of the total produce resulting from a given exertion of labor and abstinence which is allotted to labor; and it will be found on consideration that any variations in the general rate of profit must be produced by variations in one or more of the three circumstances above enumerated.

An Example. In such a country as Australia the efficiency of labor is very great, owing to the large extent of fertile land; and the cost at which the necessaries of life can be obtained is for the same reason very small. The circumstances are sufficient to produce a very high rate of profit, together with a high rate of wages.

Workmen are not ultimately benefited by a rise in wages which causes their employers' profits to sink below the ordinary rate. In explaining the relation between wages and profits in the last chapter, it was said that the laborers in any particular employment derive no permanent benefit from a rise in wages which reduces their employers' profits below the ordinary rate. But it may be urged that if all the working men in such a nation as Great Britain combined in their demand for higher wages, they would be able to obtain a larger share of the wealth produced by capital and labor, and the current rate of profit prevailing in this country would be reduced. Laying aside the innumerable obstacles to such perfect organization and unanimity among all classes of workmen which such a demand would require, let it be supposed that a universal demand for higher wages takes place throughout the United Kingdom, that the demand is conceded, that profits are decreased, and that the rate of interest is reduced from 3½ to 2 percent. Such a reduction would tend in two ways to reduce the wages fund, and therefore ultimately to produce a fall in wages. The higher the rate of interest the greater is the inducement to save. A fall in the rate of interest from 3½ to 2 percent would cause many persons to expend their wealth in their own enjoyments rather than employ it productively as capital. A reward of £2 a year for every £100 which they abstain from spending would not be sufficient in a great many instances to induce persons to save. Hence, the supply of capital would be checked. On the other hand, there are many persons who would say, "We cannot live on the income yielded by 2 percent on our capital; as we cannot get more than this here we will invest in some foreign enterprise, in an Indian tea garden, an American railway, or a Peruvian mine." A large amount of capital is consequently exported, while at the same time the accumulation of capital is checked by decreasing the inducement to save. Such circumstances would gradually produce a very great diminution in the capital of the country. Circulating capital always bears some proportion to the gross amount of capital. As previously explained in Section I, Capital is divided into Fixed Capital and Circulating Capital. If, therefore, the capital of a country is diminished, both these portions of it will in all probability be reduced. The principal employment of circulating capital is the maintenance of laborers; that is, paying the wages of labor. A decrease in the amount of circulating capital will therefore inevitably produce a decrease in the wages of labor. Hence, it is seen that any circumstance which materially reduces the rate of interest in a country checks the accumulation of capital, and leads to the export of capital. The capital of the country is thereby reduced, circulating capital is diminished, and wages fall.

If the rate of interest is unduly decreased by the demand of laborers for higher wages, the sufferings of the working classes when the consequent reduction of circulating capital takes place will probably be very acute. The increased wages which for a time they were able to secure would have stimulated a considerable increase of population. When, therefore, the reduction of wages takes place, the laborers find that their numbers have increased, and that their means of subsistence are diminished. Misfortune comes upon them like a two-edged sword that cuts both ways. The laboring population of the east end of London was a few years since suffering under this double calamity. The expenses which a working man necessarily incurs are much larger in London than in most places; house rent and fuel are dear, and the rates are extremely high; the wages of laborers are therefore necessarily higher in London than in such a place as Glasgow. The consequence of this has been that one of the principal trades of the east end of London, shipbuilding, was for a time carried on by capitalists at a comparative loss; it has consequently been gradually removed from London to such ports as Glasgow, where labor and the requisite materials can be obtained cheaper than in London. During the time in which high wages were being realized by the London workmen a large increase of population was stimulated, and the miseries produced by the subsequent stagnation of trade were thus greatly aggravated.

The Export of Capital widens the area of Competition. The principal effect of the export of capital upon profits is that it widens the area of competition. It has been said that when the profits realized in a particular trade are exceptionally high, the competition of other capitalists gradually reduces profits to the ordinary rate. If this is true between one trade and another in the same country, it is also true, though in a more limited degree, between one country and another. Competition is not so active between different countries, because in many cases the export of capital would be attended by great loss and inconvenience. A shopkeeper in London may find his expenses so heavy that, when he has deducted wages for superintendence and compensation for risk, his capital only returns him an interest of 2 percent. He may at the same time be well aware that the interest on capital in Australia is 10 percent, and yet there may be insuperable obstacles to prevent him from entering into business in Australia. The difficulty of obtaining authentic information respecting the best way of investing his money in that country, the distance which he would have to travel, the expense he would incur if he determined upon emigrating, and many other minor considerations, would very probably be sufficient to deter him from leaving his own country or investing in foreign enterprises. The obstacles which have hitherto to a large extent prevented the export of capital are gradually becoming less powerful. As intelligence is more widely diffused, and the means of locomotion and communication are improved, the export of capital will in all probability steadily increase. In many parts of the Continent there are a great number of manufactures which are carried on by Englishmen with English capital. A large firm of stocking manufacturers at Nottingham have a branch of their business established in Saxony. If by a strike their workmen in England should succeed in getting such wages as to reduce the profits of the Nottingham trade below those realized in Saxony, the heads of the firm would no doubt take every opportunity of reducing the Nottingham business and increasing the manufacture of stockings in Saxony. In other words, there would be an export of fixed and circulating capital from England to Saxony. Such a phenomenon as a manufacturer carrying on his business in a foreign country was almost unknown a century ago, but it will in all probability become more and more common until the rate of profit realized in different countries is more nearly similar than it now is.

The three great divisions into which wealth is divided have now been investigated; this section cannot, however, be brought to a close without explaining the effect of trades' unions, strikes, and cooperation upon wages and profits. This explanation will form the subject of the following chapter.

QUESTIONS ON CHAPTER III. *THE PROFITS OF CAPITAL*

1. What is the real nature of the profits of capital?
2. Show by an example that profits are just and should be perpetual.
3. Of what three elements are the profits of capital composed?
4. What is the interest on capital, and how can the rate of interest in any country at any particular time be ascertained?
5. Why does the rate of profit vary in different trades?
6. Explain the effect of insecurity of property upon profits.
7. Is the rate of interest variable in the same country and at the same time?
8. Why does the rate of interest decline as population increases?
9. Give an illustration showing that the rate of interest declines as the margin of cultivation descends.

10. It is sometimes said that profits depend on the rate of wages; explain why this is inaccurate, and state on what profits really depend.
11. Do high prices necessarily denote large profits?
12. Give an example showing that higher prices are sometimes accompanied by a decline in the rate of profit.
13. On what three variables does the cost of labor to the capitalist depend?
14. In what two ways does a reduction of the rate of interest in any particular country tend to decrease the national capital?
15. Explain the effect of such a decrease on the condition of the laboring classes.
16. What therefore is the effect of the export of capital upon profits?
17. Why does competition act more slowly between different countries than between different trades in the same country?
18. Why is the export of capital likely to increase?
    (a) How can the fact be accounted for that the profits of a speculator on the stock exchange are larger than the profits of farming?
    (b) Is usury wicked? Were the laws regulating the rate of profit any good?
    (e) What effect has the export of English capital on the rate of profit in England?
    (d) Suppose the whole laboring population of the world by a combination succeeded in obtaining wages so large that capital was deprived of any share of the wealth it assisted to produce; what effect would this have on production, and on the welfare of the entire community?
    (e) Show that a high rate of profit sometimes indicates that a country is in a satisfactory condition, and sometimes the reverse. Illustrate this by the United States and Mexico.

CHAPTER FOUR

On Trades' Unions, Strikes, and Cooperative Societies

The Functions of a Trade's Union explained. A Trade's Union is a society formed by the workmen engaged in any particular trade; this society generally fulfills the double purpose of a benefit club and an organization for protecting the interests of the workmen by obtaining for them the highest possible rate of wages. The utility of trades' unions as benefit clubs is undeniable. Each member of a trade's union is compelled by the rules of his society to contribute a certain weekly sum to its funds. In the case of illness or loss of work he obtains assistance from these funds, and in the case of his death his family receives a certain sum of money from the same source. In point of fact a trade's union is an assurance company. The assistance which trades' unions render to workmen is so considerable, that no members of such unions as the Amalgamated Carpenters and Joiners', or the Amalgamated Engineers',[1] are ever known to be in receipt of parish relief.

The other function of a trade's union, namely, that of protecting the interests of workmen by obtaining for them the highest possible rate of wages, is that by which unionism is best known, and it is this which has made it so extremely unpopular with the capitalist classes. For though unions are not necessarily connected with strikes, a strike could not be successfully carried on without some such organization as a trade's union supplies.

Strikes. Notwithstanding the loss which workmen and employers have frequently suffered in consequence of strikes, few would now assert that workmen have not the right to join an association for the protection of what they believe to be their interests. Let us inquire what a strike really is. It is neither more nor less than a refusal on the part of workmen to sell their labor on the terms offered by those who desire to buy it. No one thinks a corn merchant or any other trader is culpable if he refuses to sell his goods at the price offered by his customers. If it be justifiable for a merchant to refuse the terms offered by those who wish to buy his commodities, it cannot be wrong for a workman to do the same; and if it be right for one man to refuse to work on the terms offered by his employer, it cannot be wrong for ten, a hundred, or a thousand men, to do the same. The conduct of workmen in striking for higher wages, or to resist a reduction, may be either prudent or imprudent, but it can never deserve censure as morally wrong. "Everyone has a right to do all that he wills, provided he infringes not the equal freedom of any other person." If this moral law had always been observed by trades' unionists they would have deprived their enemies of all semblance of an argument against the right of combination. This law is constantly violated by all classes of the community, and workmen have not herein shown themselves superior to the rest of humanity. They have not generally been content with the right of combination, but they have used force and violence to compel those workmen to join their societies, who would otherwise have been unwilling to become members of trades' unions. Constant annoyances, bodily violence, and even murder, are weapons which trades' unionists have not scorned to employ in order to prevent the competition of non-unionist workmen and workwomen. Such conduct deserves the strongest censure, and those who commit or sanction it are deserving of the severest punishment, but it does not touch the right of freedom of combination, which is all that rational upholders of trades' unions contend for.

The fact that some men abuse the power which this right confers affords no reason why all should be deprived of it.

Some of the means employed by Unionists to obtain high wages explained. It has been said that the object of a trade's union is to obtain for its members the highest possible rate of wages. Although trades' unionists are often accused of setting at defiance every principle of political economy, they are good enough economists to know that the rate of wages depends on the proportion between the sum paid as wages and the number of those between whom this sum is distributed. It is true that they do not generally apply this important principle to the whole of the wages-receiving class, but they do, as unionists, apply it to the particular trade in which they happen to be employed. Many of the rules of trades' unions are, therefore, designed with the purpose of reducing or restricting the number of workmen employed in the trade. For instance, no shipwright can become a member of a union who has not served a seven years' apprenticeship; and no employer can engage a shipwright who cannot produce the indentures of his apprenticeship, because, if he did so, all the unionist workmen in his employment would strike. Again, in the hat trade, no master workman may have more than two apprentices at the same time. A practical restriction is also placed upon the number of bricklayers, because no master mason (as the first-class workman is called) will do any work whatever, unless a laborer is also employed to work under him.

A comparison of the restrictive Rules of Trades' Unions with the Etiquette of the Learned Professions. It is curious to observe that the rules of trades' unions just quoted have a remarkably exact parallel in the rules prevailing in the learned professions of medicine and the law. No shipwright will work in the same yard with a man who cannot produce the indentures of his apprenticeship. No doctor will meet in consultation one who has not received the degree of some recognized licensing body. Until 1878 all the licensing bodies in England refused to admit women to their degrees, and the competition in the medical profession was by this means restricted. The admission of women to the medical and other degrees of the London

University was at last carried in spite of the opposition of the great majority of medical graduates of the University. In a similar way there have frequently been strikes against the admittance of women into certain trades, such as china painting, carpet weaving, etc.; the object being to limit the competition for employment in the trade. No hatter may have more than two apprentices at the same time. No solicitor may have more than two pupils in his office at the same time. No master mason will work without an inferior under him. No Queen's Counsel will go into court without a junior barrister with him. This curious resemblance is not quoted in defense of the restrictive rules of trades' unions, but merely to show that the learned and the unlearned have resorted to the same means for protecting the interests of their own profession or trade. No doubt both believe that these restrictions are good for themselves in particular and for the community in general. But if the restrictions are unjustifiable in the one instance, they must be so in the other.

There are Combinations among Employers as well as among Workmen. There are trades' unions in a great many businesses and professions which are called by other names. Some of the opponents of unionism overlook the fact that combinations are formed by the employers as well as by the employed. The ironmasters, for instance, have their quarterly meetings at which they agree upon the wages to be offered for particular sorts of work during the ensuing three months. When they resolve upon a reduction of wages, they agree that the alteration shall be simultaneous throughout the whole district; just as workmen, in any trade, agree to strike work on a particular day, when they are contending for higher wages.

Trade Combinations imply hostility: while this remains strikes and lockouts will continue to occur. The combinations existing among employers are justifiable on exactly the same grounds as the combinations of workmen. The hostility which such combinations imply may be deplorable, it certainly leads to much misery and pecuniary loss; but while the hostility remains no good can be done by attacking the right of combination. Trades' unions, and associations of employers, would not exist in their present form, unless there were an antagonism of interest between workmen and their employers. Those, therefore, who most deplore the frequency of strikes, and the misery and heartburnings they produce, should endeavor to remove the antagonism of interest between employers and employed, of which strikes and lockouts are only the outward and visible signs. A "lockout" is really a strike of the masters. The men make some demand for shorter hours or for higher wages, which the employers refuse to grant. The men persisting in their demand, the employers throughout the district discharge all their workmen. Their gates are closed; and production is entirely suspended, until one or other of the parties gives way, or until some compromise is agreed to by both.

Cooperation. Many schemes have been of late propounded, with the view of removing the present antagonism between capital and labor, by making employers and employed feel that their interests are in the main identical. The fundamental principle of all these schemes is that workmen should have a direct pecuniary interest in the prosperity of the trade in which they are engaged; this interest is created by the workmen owning the whole or some part of the capital which their industry requires. Cooperative trading societies are those in which the workmen employed own the whole of the capital necessary for carrying on their business. In such cases it is evident that the antagonism between employers and employed ceases to exist, because both capital and labor are provided by the same individuals. There are several cooperative trading societies in Great Britain, but the most successful and consequently the best known of these institutions are in Paris. In the year 1852 seventeen masons, in Paris, resolved to carry on business with the aid of no other capital than that which they themselves could provide. They at first created a small capital by saving one-tenth of their daily earnings. With this small beginning they commenced business, and so successful were they, that in 1860 the society consisted of 107 members with a capital of £14,500. Many most important buildings in Paris have been built by this society. Every laborer employed in this society owns part of the capital. The ordinary wages are paid and the profits of the capital are distributed in the following manner: two-fifths are reserved to pay the annual dividend on the capital, and the remaining three-fifths are distributed as a bonus upon labor. The amount of the bonus which each laborer receives is proportioned to the amount of work which he has done during the year. By this arrangement perfect identity of interest is established between capital and labor, and, at the same time, the earnings of each individual are proportionate to the amount of capital which he has in the concern, and upon the quantity of labor which he performs. Another most remarkable cooperative society in Paris is that of the housepainters. This society was founded by M. Leclaire, the son of a poor village shoemaker who in his 20th year was working as a laborer upon wages of 3s. a day. From this humble beginning he quickly succeeded in raising himself to be the head of a large business. This in itself is no uncommon circumstance; but Leclaire was a very uncommon man, for instead of being content with the personal enjoyment of the wealth he had thus honorably earned, he set himself to devise a scheme to enable all his workmen to become his partners. "I asked myself," he says in his account of his life, "could a workman in our business, by putting more heart into his work, produce in the same lapse of time—i.e., a day—a surplus of work equivalent to the value of an hour's pay, i.e., 6d? Could he, besides, save 2½ d. a day by avoiding all waste of the materials as trusted to him, and by taking greater care of his tools?" If these questions could be answered in the affirmative Leclaire foresaw a clear extra profit of more than £3000 a year. (He employed three hundred men and there were three hundred working days in the year.) He did answer these questions in the affirmative, and the result showed that he was right. He divided his profits with his workmen for the first time in 1841, and the sum thus annually divided increased very rapidly as the scheme began to take effect in stimulating the zeal and trustworthiness of the laborers. The plan adopted was this: there was a mutual aid society established among Leclaire's workmen which at first was almost identical with an ordinary benefit society. The capital of this society grew and increased and was invested in the business: hence the mutual aid society became a partner, as it were, and all its members participated in the profits. The society has made steady progress from its beginning; it was so judiciously organized by Leclaire that his death which occurred in 1872 did not interfere with its prosperity. In 1877 or 5 years after Leclaire's death the capital of the firm had increased to £40,000 and the business done in that year was £80,000. The total amount distributed as the men's share in the profits between 1842 and 1877 was £80,000. The number of men among whom the distribution was made in 1877 was 984.[2] The cooperative principle was applied with great success to agriculture, by the late Mr. Gurdon, of Assington, Suffolk. About 50 years ago Mr. Gurdon let some farms to an association of laborers; he advanced them the necessary capital, which they agreed to repay in a certain number of years. The experiment has proved entirely successful; the farms are in a high state of cultivation; Mr. Gurdon's capital has long since been repaid, and the condition of the laborers has improved in the most striking manner. The laborers appoint from among their own body a committee of management, and those who are employed receive the ordinary agricultural wages, and at the end of the year the profits are divided among all who own shares.

Copartnership. In England a modification of cooperative principles has been carried out in several instances, with great success. One of the best known of these copartnerships of industry was that which was started by the Messrs. Briggs, of Methley near Leeds. These gentlemen had long been large colliery proprietors; they were so harassed by constant disputes with the miners, and had suffered so much pecuniary loss from the frequency of strikes, that their profits were very seriously reduced, and they were almost determined upon relinquishing their business. They however finally resolved upon trying, as a last resource, the effect of a partnership between capital and labor. They accordingly converted their business into a joint-stock company, the capital of which was £135,000, in 9000 shares of £15 each. The Messrs. Briggs retained six thousand of these shares, and the remaining three thousand shares were offered to the men employed in the mines. These shares were quickly taken up, and thus a workman, even if he owned but one share, was virtually a partner in the concern. The company is managed by directors, by whom all the shareholders are represented, the workmen appointing one of their own body. When the profits on capital exceed 10 percent, it has been agreed that half the surplus should be distributed as a bonus upon labor, each workman receiving a sum proportionate to the wages he has earned during the previous year. This scheme worked with great success for nearly ten years; during a time when disputes between employers and employed in the surrounding district were bitter, when strikes were frequent and heavy losses were being made, the business of the Messrs. Briggs was most prosperous, and the relations between them and their men were harmonious and friendly. It has, however, unfortunately happened that the principle of copartnership which weathered the storm of adverse times and slack trade, was not proof against the trial of a very large and sudden increase in the profits and wages in the coal trade. In the years 1871 and 1872, the degree of prosperity in the coal trade was quite unprecedented. Wages and profits were almost doubled. Under these circumstances a dispute arose at Methley on the manner and the proportion in which these greatly increased profits should be distributed between capital and labor; and the dispute resulted in the abandonment of the copartnership principle.

Although the experiment tried at Methley has been abandoned, it should be remembered that the circumstances under which it was given up were very exceptional. Copartnership has been adopted with uninterrupted success in several other departments of industry; for example, by the Messrs. Crossley in their large carpet manufactory at Halifax, and by the late Lord George Manners on a farm which he cultivated near Newmarket.

The advantages of cooperation and copartnership may be divided into two classes. In the first place, strikes are avoided, and consequently great pecuniary loss is prevented. In the second place, the efficiency of labor is greatly increased, and consequently more wealth is produced. A workman too often has the feeling that it makes no difference to him whether he is industrious or idle, careless or careful of his employer's property. He and his employer look upon each other as natural enemies, one of whom tries to do as little work and get as much wages as possible, and the other tries to give as little wages and to get as much work as possible. In such a condition of things overlookers have to be engaged by the employer, to see that the workmen fulfill their share of the bargain; but however much they are overlooked average men will never work with the best energy they can give, unless they feel that they themselves are directly benefited by their own labor. The stimulus which copartnership gives to labor is too often overlooked. Every capitalist who has given copartnership a fair trial in his own business, is always ready to admit that it is most profitable in a pecuniary sense. The bonus distributed among the workmen does not represent so much taken away from the employer's profits; it represents part of the pecuniary value of the increased efficiency of labor.

We are constantly assured that strikes have imperiled and still threaten to destroy the commercial greatness of England. Strikes can never be prevented by discouraging trades' unions by adverse legislation. That plan has been tried for half a century, and strikes have become more and more frequent. Strikes are the result of the antagonism between capital and labor. Remove the antagonism, and strikes will die a natural death.

Boards of Arbitration. In some industries, especially in the lace and hosiery trades of Nottingham, the establishment of boards of arbitration has been most successful in preventing strikes. These boards are composed of an equal number of workmen and employers; they meet every month, and all disputes between masters and men are submitted to the arbitration of the boards. Nothing can be more beneficial than the operation of these boards when once a dispute has arisen; and by promoting friendly intercourse between employers and employed, they may have some influence in preventing disputes; but it must be borne in mind that they deal with the symptom—the strike, and not with its cause—the antagonism of interest. They cannot therefore be regarded as complete and efficient remedies for strikes.

Cooperative Stores. Some misapprehension may arise by confusing cooperation with the so-called "cooperative" stores which have lately become so popular in London and other large towns. The real nature of cooperation is a union between capital and labor. In such institutions as the Civil Service Store in the Haymarket, there is not necessarily any connection between capital and labor. It is a joint-stock company, the shares of which are owned, for the most part, by those who do not contribute by their labor to the success of the store. The shopmen and superintendents may own shares, but it is not an essential part of the undertaking that they should do so. A cooperative store relies for its success, not on a union of capital and labor, but mainly upon the ready-money principle. The "cooperation" which exists in a store is not a cooperation between capital and labor; but between the consumer and the distributor. The prices of commodities sold in a cooperative store are less than those charged in an ordinary shop, because no bad debts are made, no expensive advertising need be resorted to, no costly shopfronts need be kept up, and the cost of carriage of goods sold is not borne by the proprietors of the business. There is no reason, except the difficulty of overcoming the prejudice against anything new, why nearly all tradesmen should not conduct their businesses on the same principles as a cooperative store. The oldest and most celebrated of cooperative stores is that of the Rochdale Pioneers. In this society the ready-money principle is strictly adhered to, and the goods are sold at the ordinary retail prices. The accounts are made up quarterly, and the profits are divided in the following manner; 5 percent per annum is allowed as interest on the shareholders' capital, and the remainder is divided among the purchasers, each customer receiving an amount proportionate to the sum which he has expended in purchasing commodities at the store. The Rochdale Pioneers' Society, which was started by workmen, and began in 1844 with sufficient capital only to buy one chest of tea and a hogshead of sugar, now does a business of £250,000 a year. There can therefore be no doubt that, when skillfully managed, cooperative stores are capable of achieving very striking financial success.

The advantages which cooperative stores afford to their customers are undoubted. It is therefore probable that the principle of ready-money payments, the main cause of the success of cooperative stores, will, in time, become general in many branches of trade.

QUESTIONS ON CHAPTER IV. *TRADES' UNIONS, STRIKES,*
AND COOPERATIVE SOCIETIES

1. What is a trade's union?
2. What two functions does a trade's union usually fulfill?
3. Why are trades' unions unpopular with the capitalist classes?
4. What is the connection between trades' unions and strikes?
5. What is a strike?
6. Can it be shown that men have no right to strike?
7. In what respect has the conduct of trades' unionists frequently been blameworthy?
8. Explain some of the rules by means of which trades' unionists have endeavored to raise the wages given in their own employments.
9. Describe the similarity between the rules of trades' unions and the etiquette of the medical and legal professions.
10. Give an instance of the combination of employers, and show that their right to combine for the protection of their interests is as incontestable as that of their employees.
11. Show that no good can be done by attacking the right of combination.
12. What is the real cause of strikes and lockouts?
13. How can this cause be removed?
14. Describe cooperation, and give an example of its successful working.
15. What is copartnership? Give an illustration.
16. Do copartnerships involve any pecuniary sacrifice on the part of the employers?
17. What are the special advantages of copartnership?
18. What is a cooperative store? Upon what principle is it based?
19. Why can lower prices be charged in a cooperative store than in an ordinary shop?
20. Give a brief account of the Rochdale Pioneers' store.
    (*a*) Write an exercise describing the advantages which workmen obtain from combination, and point out that in driving a bargain with their employer it is only by means of combination that they can place themselves in a position fully to protect their own interests.

(*b*) If you were a member of a trade's union, and a strike were resolved upon, would you advise that the strike should be commenced when trade was active or when it was dull?

(*c*) Do you think cooperative stores do harm to the interests of the community because they injure the retail grocers and other tradesmen? And if not, why not?

ON FOREIGN COMMERCE, CREDIT, AND TAXATION

THIS SECTION COMPRISES CHAPTERS ON FOREIGN COMMERCE, CREDIT AND its influence on prices, and Taxation. It will perhaps appear that foreign commerce and credit should have been explained in the section headed "The Exchange of Wealth." It however seems that in a short and elementary treatise there are many advantages in separating the subjects usually comprised under the head "The Exchange of Wealth." A knowledge of the meaning of value and price, of the causes which regulate the prices of commodities, and of the true nature of money, is essential to a right understanding of the causes which determine the respective amounts of rent, wages and profits. At the same time the subjects of foreign commerce and credit, if introduced prior to the consideration of the distribution of wealth, might have wearied and perplexed the beginner. These subjects have therefore been reserved for the fourth and last section.

CHAPTER ONE

ON FOREIGN COMMERCE

A DEVELOPMENT OF FOREIGN COMMERCE ENSURES DIVISION OF LABOR. The great advantage derived from foreign commerce is that which is obtained by division of labor. If countries trade freely with each other, the natural consequence is that each nation gradually increases the production of those commodities for the manufacture of which circumstances have specially adapted it; at the same time it decreases the manufacture of those commodities which it has no particular facilities for producing. In this way the cost of production is diminished, and capital and labor work with their maximum efficiency. Take an example: France has great natural advantages for the manufacture of wine; her climate and the habits of her people cause the cultivation of the vine to be carried on with great success. Such countries as France, therefore, produce not only sufficient wine to supply their own wants, but also enough to satisfy the demand of countries like England, the climate of which is unsuited to the cultivation of the vine. The advantage of foreign trade is that we can get from foreign countries either what we could not produce at all for ourselves; or else we get commodities in exchange for a smaller expenditure of labor and capital than it would cost us to produce them ourselves.

Protection is disastrous to the general interests of the community. The salt mines of Cheshire and those existing in Salzburg and other parts of Germany, give to that country and to England special advantages for the production of salt. In the absence of protective duties probably all the salt required in France would be provided by England and Germany; the salt procured in Northwich and Droitwich is of excellent quality and requires comparatively so little labor to render it fit for use that it may be almost regarded as a free gift of nature. This salt can therefore be sold at a very low price, while at the same time it is superior in quality to that produced by the more elaborate processes employed to manufacture salt in France. In a word English salt is both better and cheaper than French salt, and would command the market if the trade were free. But the French protectionist says: "This must not be, there is a large class of industrious people in France engaged in the industry of making salt, and a branch of our home trade would be destroyed if English salt were admitted into France duty free. We must levy so large an import duty on English salt as to bring up its price to something in excess of the price of the salt produced in France, this will keep English salt out of France and encourage a branch of native industry." This is accordingly done: a heavy import duty is levied on foreign salt, which is thus kept out of the market. It is quite true that this policy "protects" the salt trade in France; that is, it induces a certain amount of the disposable capital and labor of France to engage in a trade which is comparatively unproductive of wealth. What the protectionist forgets, however, is that if the protection were withdrawn and the unproductive trade in consequence ceased to exist, the capital and labor engaged in it would not remain idle; they would seek some other employment in which the wealth produced would be a sufficient recompense without the adventitious aid of protection. If the salt manufacturers of France were undersold by the salt manufacturers of England, the former might for a time suffer pecuniary loss; but the ultimate result would be that they would gradually withdraw their labor and capital from a comparatively unremunerative trade, and employ them in some other industry, for which France possesses exceptional advantages. Thus there is no loss, but a transfer of capital and labor from a comparatively unremunerative employment to one in which they would work with greatly increased efficiency. In such a case, the total production of wealth is increased, and the national capital consequently augmented.

An illustration of this transfer of capital and labor from one kind of industry to another may be seen in what is happening now in English agriculture, in the face of the recent large imports of food from America. The English farmer is being undersold by the American farmer in regard to a large number of commodities, such as wheat and cheese. The English farmer does not cry out for protection; but he casts about to discover what kinds of crops he can still produce where he can hold his own against the Americans. The next few years will probably see a great many farms turned into huge market gardens, because fresh flowers, fruit and vegetables cannot be so largely imported as the less perishable commodities just referred to. A movement has already begun in this direction; and it should be remembered that the general body of consumers, having to spend less for their necessaries, such as bread and cheese, will have more to spend upon such luxuries as flowers and fruit.

The cost of Protection to the consumer. This leads to a consideration of the effect of protection upon the consumers of the commodities produced in the protected trades. Protectionists have usually no consideration whatever for the consumers. They busy themselves much in protecting the producers, but they never consider the consumers: and it must be remembered that if the article protected is a necessary of life, to overlook the interests of the consumer for the supposed benefit of the producer, is to prefer the well-being of a part to the well-being of the whole. Let us consider what is the effect of the protective duty on salt in France upon the entire body of the French people. In the first place they have to put up with an inferior article. This is a disadvantage which it is hardly possible to measure in money, but it is nevertheless a very real and distinct disadvantage, for besides the annoyance of having coarse and gritty salt at table there is also to be considered the effect of using an inferior kind of salt for agricultural and manufacturing processes. But if the pecuniary loss involved through using an inferior article cannot be accurately measured, that arising from an increase in price can be reckoned up with a very considerable degree of exactitude. Those acquainted with the trade assert that the protective duty raises the price of salt in France one halfpenny a pound. Now the annual consumption of salt in France for domestic purposes is 350,000,000 lbs., therefore the French people are fined £750,000 every year in the extra price they pay for their salt; and no one is one half-penny the better; for this £750,000 is a measure of the natural disadvantages the French producers of salt labor under compared to the English producers of salt. It is as if a man had a beautiful spring of water close to his door but situated in his neighbor's garden: the neighbor says he may take all he likes for a rent of £4 a year, he will not however accept his offer because he has a spring of his own. But his own spring is a mile away and the water is not so good; moreover instead of getting all he wants for £4 a year he has to pay a boy 3s. a week or £7. 16s. a year in order to bring him one pail of water every day. He therefore fines himself in three ways. He has an inferior kind of water; he has less of it; and he pays £3. 16s. more for it. And no one is benefited by this expenditure, not even the boy who gets the 3s. a week; he could earn 6d. a day in a hundred different ways quite as easily as he earns it by carrying the water, the 6d. a day is no more than a bare compensation to him for the labor he endures; no favor is conferred on him; he gives full value for what he receives.

The effect of Protection on Wages. We have now traced the effect of protection on the prices of protected commodities: it is almost invariably the case in protectionist countries that among the protected articles there are many of the daily necessaries of life. Where this is so, protection decreases the wages of labor; the real reward of the laborer is diminished because his money wages will exchange for a smaller quantity of commodities. And on the other hand free trade by decreasing prices tends to increase the real reward of the laborer, and confers a direct benefit upon thousands of people. If any necessary of life is cheapened one of two things must occur, either the cost of production is decreased, or the real reward of the laborer is increased. If wages remain the same, after the price of a necessary is decreased, the real reward of the laborer is augmented, because his money wages will exchange for a larger quantity of commodities. If, on the other hand, wages are decreased in proportion to the increased cheapness of a necessary, the real reward of the laborer remains the same, while the cost of production is decreased. It is therefore evident that the benefits attending a decrease in the price of any of the necessaries of life are much more general in their operation than the supposed benefit which is conferred upon producers by protecting them against foreign competition. A decrease in the price of a commodity also leads to an increased accumulation of capital; for the expenditure of consumers being reduced they have greater opportunity of saving, and a larger amount of wealth is consequently employed as capital. In striving to protect the producers of a commodity, protectionists thus inflict a much deeper injury upon the whole community than at first sight appears.

An illustration of the effect of a Bounty for the encouragement of Native Industry. At the present time hardly any fine white sugar is made in England; the English consumers are supplied almost entirely from France. The reason of this is not that French sugar is better, or naturally cheaper than what was formerly manufactured in England. It can, however, be sold at a cheaper rate because the French government give what virtually amounts to a bounty on all the sugar exported from France. This bounty enables the French sugar refiners to undersell their English competitors, and consequently nearly all the large sugar refineries which used to exist on the Clyde and at Bristol have been shut up, and the labor and capital which they employed are being transferred to other industries. It is thus seen that no *permanent* injury is inflicted on English industry by the policy of the French government; but that the simple result of the protection they afford to their home industry is that the whole French nation is taxed in order to enable the whole English nation to obtain sugar at less than cost price.

The arguments of Protectionists applied to the introduction of Steam Carriage. The plea of protection might have been urged with great force by the owners and drivers of stagecoaches at the time of the introduction of railway traveling: they might have said that these newfangled railroads would cause many hundreds of people to be thrown out of employment; that coach proprietors and the owners of roadside inns would be ruined, that the national character would deteriorate, and that the race of horses would in a few years become extinct. All this very possibly was said, but with no avail. The coach drivers and proprietors and the innkeepers were a very small body compared with the rest of the community; the good of the many was preferred to the profit of the few; and a wonderful development of commerce and other innumerable advantages derived from railway traveling have resulted.

The Candlemakers' Petition. M. Bastiat, in the following witty sketch, has placed in strong relief the absurdity of protection.

THE CANDLEMAKERS' PETITION.[1]

Petition of the Manufacturers of Candles, Waxlights, Lamps, Candlesticks, Street Lamps, Snuffers, Extinguishers, and of the producers of Oil, Tallow, Resin, Alcohol, and generally of everything connected with Lighting.

To Messieurs the Members of the Chamber of Deputies Gentlemen,

We are suffering from the intolerable competition of a foreign rival, placed, it would seem, in a condition so far superior to ours for the production of light, that he absolutely inundates our national market *with it at a price fabulously reduced. The moment he shows himself our trade leaves us—all consumers apply to him; and a branch of native industry, having countless ramifications, is all at once rendered completely stagnant. This rival, who is no other than the Sun, wages war to the knife against us, and we suspect that he has been raised up by perfidious Albion; inasmuch as he displays towards that haughty island a circumspection with which he dispenses in our case.*

What we pray for is, that it may please you to pass a law ordering the shutting up of all Windows, Skylights, Dormer Windows, Outside and Inside Shutters, Curtains, Blinds, Bull's-eyes; in a word of all Openings, Holes, Chinks, Clefts, and Fissures, by or through which the light of the Sun has been allowed to enter houses, to the prejudice of the meritorious manufactures with which we flatter ourselves we have accommodated our country—a country which, in gratitude, ought not to abandon us now to a strife so unequal.

We urge the following reasons in support of our request. First: if you shut up as much as possible all access to natural light, and create a demand for artificial light, which of our French manufactures will not be encouraged by it?

If more tallow is consumed, then there must be more oxen and sheep; and consequently we shall behold the increase of artificial meadows, meat, wool, hides; and, above all, manure, which is the basis and foundation of all agricultural wealth.

If more oil is consumed, then we shall have an extended cultivation of the poppy, of the olive, and of colewort. These rich and exhausting plants will come at a right time to enable us to avail ourselves of the increased fertility which the rearing of additional cattle will impart to our lands.

Our heaths will be covered with resinous trees. Numerous swarms of bees will, on the mountains, gather perfumed treasures, now wasting their fragrance on the desert air, like the flowers from which they are derived. No branch of agriculture but will then exhibit a cheering development.

The same remark applies to navigation. Thousands of vessels will proceed to the whale fishery, and in a short time we shall possess a navy capable of maintaining the honor of France, and gratifying the patriotic aspirations of your petitioners.

But what shall we say of the manufacture of articles de Paris? *Henceforth you will behold gildings, bronzes, crystals, in candlesticks, in lamps, in lusters, in candelabra, shining forth in spacious ware-rooms, compared with which those of the present day can be regarded but as mere shops.*

No poor Resinier *from his heights on the seacoast, no coalminer from the depth of his sable gallery, but will rejoice in higher wages and increased prosperity.*

Only have the goodness to reflect, Gentlemen, and you will be convinced that there is perhaps no Frenchman, from the wealthy coal master to the humblest vendor of lucifer matches, whose lot will not be ameliorated by the success of our Petition. If you urge that the light of the Sun is a gratuitous gift of nature, and that to reject such gifts is to reject wealth itself, under pretense of encouraging the means of acquiring it, we would caution you *against giving a death blow to your own policy. Remember you have hitherto always repelled foreign products, because they approximate, more nearly than home products, to the character of gratuitous gifts. To comply with the exactions of other monopolists, you have only half a motive; and to refuse us, simply because we stand on a stronger vantage-ground than others, would be to adopt the equation, $+ \times + = -$; in other words, it would be to heap absurdity upon absurdity.*

Nature and human labor cooperate in various proportions (depending on countries and climates) in the production of commodities. The part which nature executes is always gratuitous; it is the part executed by human labor which constitutes value and is paid for. If a Lisbon orange sells for half the price of a Paris orange, it is because natural, and therefore gratuitous, heat does for the one what artificial, and consequently expensive, heat must do for the other. When an orange comes to us from Portugal, we may conclude that it is furnished in part gratuitously, in part for an onerous consideration; in other words, it comes to us half-price as compared with those of Paris.

Now it is precisely the gratuitous half (pardon the word) which we contend should be excluded. You say, How can national labor sustain competition with foreign labor, when the former has all the work to do, and the latter only does one half, the Sun supplying the remainder? But if this half, being gratuitous, determines you to exclude competition, how should the whole, being gratuitous, induce you to admit competition ? If you were consistent, you would, while excluding as hurtful to native industry, what is half gratuitous, exclude a fortiori *and with double zeal, that which is altogether gratuitous. Once more, when products such as coal, iron, corn or textile fabrics are sent us from abroad, and we can acquire them with less labor than if we made them ourselves, the difference is a free gift conferred upon us. The gift is more or less considerable in proportion as the difference is more or less great. . . . It is as perfect and complete as it can be when the donor (like the Sun in furnishing us with light) asks us for nothing. The question, and we ask it formally, is this: do you desire for our country the benefit of gratuitous consumption, or the pretended advantages of onerous production? Make your choice, but be logical; for as long as you exclude foreign fabrics, in proportion as their price approximates to* zero, *what inconsistency would it be to admit the light of the Sun, the price of which is already at* zero *during the entire day!*

Foreign trade will be advantageous to both countries only when the relative cost of the commodities exchanged is different in each country. Having now explained the general principles of Free Trade, and the advantages which nations derive from foreign commerce, let us inquire into the actual effect of the exchange of commodities between two such countries as France and England. In the first place, it must be borne in mind that no profit arises from the exchange, by two countries, of one commodity for another, unless the relative cost of the two commodities is different in the two countries. Both commodities may be cheaper in the one country than in the other, but they will not be exchanged unless their relative cost is different. For instance, gloves and spirits may both be cheaper in France than in England; it may, therefore, appear evident that France will never send gloves to England in exchange for spirits; but suppose that in France four pairs of gloves are equal in value to a gallon of spirits, while in England four pairs of gloves will exchange for one gallon and a quarter of spirits. In this case a French glove merchant would gain a quarter of a gallon of spirits for every four pairs of gloves which he exchanged with England; and the exchange might accordingly take place with advantage to both countries. If, however, the relative value of gloves and spirits were the same in each country, no exchange of these commodities would take place, because the merchants conducting such an exchange would realize no profit by the transaction. If four pairs of gloves equal in value a gallon of spirits in France and in England, a French glove merchant would not seek to effect an exchange with an English spirit merchant, because he would not gain anything by so doing. It has now been proved that the relative cost of the commodities which are exchanged must be different in the two countries effecting the exchange. But the amount of difference has not yet been defined. The difference must be at least sufficient to cover the cost of conveying the commodity from the one country to the other and to leave a margin of extra profit to the exporter. For no merchant will undertake the trouble and risk of exporting a commodity to a foreign country, if the price realized by the exported commodity is such that his profit is no greater than he would have obtained by selling the commodity in his own country.

The terms of the exchange are regulated by an equalization of Demand and Supply. The minimum difference in the relative value of the commodities has been defined; but the difference may be much more than sufficient to cover the cost of carriage and to leave a small margin of profit for the exporter. Suppose for instance that a ton of coal in France will exchange for a quarter of wheat, while in England at the same time a ton of coal will only exchange for one-third of a quarter of wheat. We may assume that the English coal merchant considers himself sufficiently recompensed if, in England, a ton of coal exchanges for one-third of a quarter of wheat; but hearing that in France he could get three times as much for his coal, he resolves upon exporting it to that country. The question now arises, Will he be able to secure the whole two-thirds of a quarter of wheat, as extra profit upon every ton of coals he sends to France? In answer to this question we refer to section 2 in which it was shown that the price of a commodity is adjusted by an equalization of demand and supply. We have supposed that the English merchant sends coals to France and obtains wheat in exchange for it; by this transaction it is evident that the supply of foreign wheat in England is increased, and therefore the demand for homegrown wheat diminishes; for similar reasons the amount of coal sent to France is increased, and consequently the demand for French coal diminishes. Now it was shown in section 2, when the theory of Value was explained, that if other things remained unaltered, an increase in the demand for a commodity causes an increase in its price; and that a reduction in the demand for a commodity decreases its price. In other words, the price of a commodity is adjusted by equalizing the supply with the demand. It is evident therefore that the exchange between England and France of coal and wheat affects the price of these commodities in both countries. In England the price of coal is increased, because the demand is increased; and the price of wheat declines, because the supply is augmented. The opposite effect is produced in France; the price of coal declining, and that of wheat increasing. It is now evident that the exchange between the two countries will not be made on the same terms as were at first agreed upon. There will no longer be a difference of ⅔ of a quarter of wheat in the exchange power of coal in the two countries; in England the exchange power of coal will have increased, in France it will have diminished; and finally, if competition is quite unchecked, the difference in the price of coal and wheat in the two countries will only be sufficient to cover the cost of carriage from one country to the other, and to afford a reasonable remuneration to the capitalist for the risk and trouble which exportation entails. The price of a commodity, insofar as there is free competition among its producers, depends ultimately upon its cost of production. Cost of carriage is frequently an important element in the cost of production of imported commodities. When import and export duties are removed, the cost of the carriage is the principal cause of the difference of price of the same commodity in different countries. This is rendered more clear if the exchange is supposed to take place between two places where legislative enactments do not attempt to check the free interchange of commodities. For instance, Lancashire produces cotton goods, while Lincolnshire grows a great quantity of wheat. The difference in the relative value of wheat and cotton cloth in Lincolnshire and Lancashire would be very considerable if these counties were prevented from exchanging their commodities for those produced in other localities. As it is, however, the difference in the price of wheat and cotton in Lancashire and Lincolnshire can never be greater than suffices to cover the expense of conveying these commodities from the one county to the other. In France, previous to the revolution, the protective spirit was so active that wheat could not be sent from one province to another in that country. The consequence was that the greatest variety of prices prevailed; wheat being plentiful and cheap in one place, while at another, owing to a bad harvest, it was very scarce and extremely dear.

The manner in which the supply of an exported commodity is equalized with the demand. It is not difficult to trace the manner in which the supply of an exported commodity is equalized to the demand, by an adjustment of the price. It has been assumed that an English merchant by sending coal to France and obtaining in exchange for each ton a quarter of wheat, realizes an extremely high profit. It therefore follows that the English merchant will export as much coal to France as he can; other merchants will also do the same, in order to participate in the exceptionally high profits. In this way the supply of coal is very largely increased in France, and in order to be able to sell it the exporters are obliged to reduce its price; at the same time, owing to the reduction of the supply of coal in England, its price is raised in that country. Hence the inducement to export coal is checked in two ways. The value of coal is raised in England and depressed in France; merchants no longer obtain as much as ⅔ of a quarter of wheat more in France than in England; what they do obtain in exchange for their coal in France is ultimately only sufficient to pay the cost of carriage and to recompense them for their risk.

Reciprocity. A great deal of misapprehension exists respecting the advantage which a country obtains from foreign trade. It is said by some that there ought to be reciprocity of exchange: that, in fact, we should not consent to accept anything from a foreign country, unless that country will accept some of our manufactured commodities in return. Even the adherents of this theory would hardly like to carry it out consistently. We obtain large quantities of tea from China, for which the Chinese people demand an equivalent value of silver. They do not, as a rule, accept our merchandise in return for their tea: this may be a great mistake on the part of the Chinese, but they are the principal sufferers, and not we. The preachers of reciprocity would hardly venture to suggest that we should refuse to allow the importation of tea from China until the Chinese will accept our manufactured goods in exchange for it.

When there is an exchange between two countries, the profit of each country varies inversely with its demand for the imported goods. In the case of the exchange of commodities between two countries, the greatest profit is realized by that country whose demand for the imported commodity is the less urgent. Thus, in the case of exchange previously investigated, any increase in the demand for coal in France would cause the English importers of coal to obtain more favorable terms of exchange; the value of coal would rise, and the importers would obtain a larger quantity of goods in exchange for it. This increased value would not however be maintained, because it would attract a larger supply; if the value were permanently increased it would denote that the cost of production had increased, in consequence of the increased demand causing less productive mines to be worked.

It must be borne in mind that the direct benefits of foreign trade consist in increasing the productive powers of the world, by enabling each country to apply its capital and labor to those industries in which they will be most efficient. Insofar as this is done commodities are produced with the least possible expenditure of capital and labor. On this point Mr. Mill says,

> There is much misconception in the common notion of what commerce does for a country. When commerce is spoken of as a source of national wealth, the imagination fixes itself upon the large fortunes acquired by merchants, rather than upon the saving of price to the consumers. But the gains of merchants when they enjoy no exclusive privilege are no greater than the profits obtained by the employment of capital in the country itself. . . . Commerce is virtually a mode of cheapening production; and in all such cases the consumer is the person ultimately benefited; the dealer in the end is sure to get his profit, whether the buyer obtains much or little for his money.

Besides the economical advantages derived from foreign trade it also produces moral and intellectual effects of the greatest importance. It brings into contact with each other the inhabitants of all the nations of the world; it is the greatest of civilizing agencies, and it is the principal guarantee for the maintenance of peace. By keeping up a constant communication between widely different nations, it enables each people, by comparing its own laws, institutions and manners with those of other countries, to profit by the example or to take warning by the fate of other nations. Commerce has also taught nations that they do not profit by each other's misfortunes, but that each country has a direct interest in the welfare and prosperity of every other.

The strongest case which the opponents of free trade have ever made, is the following: If a nation engages in foreign trade the commodities which it exports will rise in value, while those which it imports will decrease in value. This is evident both from a priori reasoning and from experience. The exported commodities will become dearer because the demand for them is increased; the imported commodities become cheaper because their supply is increased. The principal exports of such a nation as America consist in the necessaries of life, such as wheat and other agricultural produce, in return for which it receives (say the protectionists) articles of luxury, such as rare wines and costly lace. Now it is urged that this foreign trade must be disadvantageous to the bulk of the population, because it increases the price of necessaries, and decreases only the price of luxuries. This argument does not touch the main advantage of foreign commerce; viz. such a division of labor, that each country produces those commodities for the manufacture of which it has peculiar and natural advantages. The result of protection in America is to withdraw a portion of her capital and labor from her most productive industries, in order to employ them in industries that are less productive. The argument cannot moreover be regarded as a fair statement of facts. The United States are at present still pursuing a policy of protection, and in no country in the world is the cost of living so heavy. Foreign articles, whether necessaries or luxuries, are mercilessly taxed; a fine of as much as 100 and 200 percent being levied on some of them. Such articles as boots and foreign clothing of all kinds, are subject to heavy imposts; and at the same time the exportation of corn and breadstuffs to Europe is carried on on a large scale.

An example of the effect of protection in America. Mr. Wells, the late Special Commissioner of the United States Revenue, issued a report in 1870, by no means favorable to the opponents of free trade. Mr. Wells' views are the more striking because when he received the appointment of Commissioner of Revenue he was a strong protectionist, and he was led to change his opinions on the subject by the facts which came under his observation during his official experience. His report showed that the tariffs imposed are so heavy as to be a most serious burden to the industry of the country. The following example shows the way in which these tariffs depress trade. Mr. Wells states that

> ...in 1869 an enterprising citizen of the Northwest visited England for the purpose of contracting for an iron vessel suitable for the grain trade of the upper lakes. As foreign-built ships are not admitted on the American registry, it was proposed to take over the vessel in sections, simply to serve as a pattern, and at the same time it was intended to import skilled workmen, and to establish an iron shipbuilding yard in the vicinity of Chicago. But when the duties, varying from 38 to 66 percent, on the various articles employed in the construction of the vessel came to be calculated, they were found to amount to so much that the project had to be abandoned. Thus Chicago and its neighborhood are still without an iron shipbuilding yard.

The whole population is taxed in the partially successful attempt to protect the interest of a few hundred American ironmasters. To such circumstances as that just narrated the commissioner attributes the decline in American shipping which has caused so much discussion in the States. Mr. Wells says that in America the cost of living is increasing in a greater ratio than the rate of wages and salaries; and he complains, not so much that comforts are curtailed, but that the power of saving is diminished. "The rich are becoming richer and the poor poorer." "Small accumulations of capital are stopped." It is perhaps not too much to assert that nothing but the extraordinary internal resources of America have enabled her so far to triumph over the self-imposed burdens on her industry. The facts just narrated show that the protectionist policy of the United States does not arise from the desire to prevent an increase in the price of the necessaries of life. The necessity of relying upon foreign countries for our supplies of food has forced upon England the adoption of free trade. This necessity does not exist in America, and consequently the recognition of the advantages of free trade is delayed. The following extract from an American paper gives some idea of one way in which protection has increased the cost of living in the United States.

> Taxes on an American when in his clothes—Hat, silk, 60 percent; ribbon, 60 percent; alpaca lining for brim, 50 cents a pound, and 35 percent; leather inside 35 percent; muslin lining 7¼ cents a square yard; glue, 20 percent. Coat—cloth, 55 cents a pound, and 35 percent *ad valorem;* silk lining, 60 percent; alpaca used therein, 50 cents a pound, and 35 percent *ad valorem;* buttons, if worsted, 20 cents a pound, and 35 percent *ad valorem;* worsted braid, 50 cents a pound, and 35 percent *ad valorem;* velvet for collar, 60 percent; red worsted padding, 50 cents a pound, and 35 percent *ad valorem;* hemp padding, 40 percent. Pantaloons—cassimere, 50 cents a pound, and 35 percent *ad valorem;* cotton used therein, 5 cents a square yard; hemp cloth for facing, 40 percent; metal buttons, 30 percent. Vest—silk or satin, 60 percent; linen lining, 35 percent; silk buttons, 60 percent. Braces, 35 percent. Undershirt—if silk, 60 percent; if worsted, 50 cents a pound, and 35 percent *ad valorem;* if cotton, 35 percent. Drawers, the same. Shirts—cotton, 5 cents a square yard; linen for the front, 35 percent. Buttons, 35 percent. Boots—raw hides, 10 percent; tanned leather, calfskin, 30 percent; if patent leather, 35 percent; soles, 35 percent. Neckerchief—if silk, 60 percent. Pocket handkerchief—if silk, 60 percent; if linen, 35 percent. Kid gloves—50 percent. Pocket knife—35 percent. Watch—25 percent. Silk watch chain—60 percent.

Exports and Imports constantly tend to an equality. Mr. Mill states this tendency thus: "The produce of a country exchanges for the produce of other countries at such values as are required in order that the whole of her exports may exactly pay for the whole of her imports." Or, as he elsewhere expresses it, "the exports and imports between two countries must in the aggregate pay for each other." It should here, however, be pointed out that though the necessity of paying for its imports is by far the most important part of a country's liabilities, yet it may besides have liabilities on account of dividends on foreign capital invested in it, etc. If there were no regular interchange of commodities between, for instance, France and England, the fact that French loans to the amount of many millions have been subscribed for, and are held in England, would necessitate an export either of ordinary merchandise or the precious metals from France to England. Hence, over and above the exports which France sends to England, equaling in value the English imports into France, France must send an equivalent for her debts to us. There is another respect in which one country may be indebted to another; when two countries exchange their respective productions, it is evident that the country which undertakes the carriage of the commodities backwards and forwards must receive an equivalent for this service. Speaking roughly, England does the carrying trade of the world; and therefore all nations with whom England trades are indebted to her for the carriage both of their exports and imports. Hence England's imports always exceed her exports, and would continue to do so, even if no foreign loans were held in England. In order to make this quite clear, we will imagine that a farmer living at Cromer wishes to exchange £20 worth of wheat for £20 worth of furniture belonging to a furniture broker at Norwich. It is arranged that the farmer sends his wheat by road from Cromer to Norwich, and that his wagon and horses are to bring back the furniture. In this case we will imagine that the carriage of the wheat and the furniture costs the farmer £2. He therefore says to the broker, "I am not going to be put to this expense and trouble without getting anything in exchange." Perhaps the broker then offers to give him £1 worth more furniture. "It will be all right then," he says; "you will get £21 worth of furniture, and you will give me £20 worth of wheat and pay the cost of carriage. That way we shall each pay half the cost of carriage." But the farmer may say, "No; by the time my wheat reaches you it has cost me £21; you ought therefore to give me £21 worth of furniture and deliver it to me at your own expense." If the farmer is a hard bargainer he will succeed in making good this demand; and he will obtain £22 worth of furniture in exchange for his £20 worth of wheat. That is to say his imports will exceed his exports by 10 percent. In the same way a country which performs the carrying trade of exports and imports, will be indemnified for this service by receiving imports of a greater value than the exports which she gives in exchange. The imports of England have for several years exceeded her exports by more than £100,000,000. The average excess of the value of our imports over our exports for the six years ending with 1874 was over £100,000,000. This excess must be regarded partly as the liquidation of cost of carriage, and partly as the interest due to the English holders of foreign securities. It may also in part be due to the withdrawal of English capital from foreign investments. The point, therefore, at which the foreign trade of a country reaches equilibrium, is not that at which the exports and imports are equal, but that at which the exports, whatever these consist of, suffice to discharge all its liabilities. The presence of counteracting circumstances does not, however, falsify the proposition originally laid down, that the exports and imports of a country *tend* to an equality. The following example will show the manner in which this tendency is exerted. Let it be supposed that the whole foreign trade of England is carried on with France, and that in a given year the exports of England to France are considerably exceeded by the imports to England from France. In such a case as this England will be, as it were, in debt to France, and this debt will have to be defrayed by an export of money from England to France; the supply of money will in this way be increased in France and decreased in England. Now it was shown in Chapter IV, Section II, that the value of money is regulated in the same way as the value of other commodities; viz. by an equalization of the demand with the supply. In France, therefore, owing to the importation of specie, the value of money will decline and prices will rise; while in England, owing to the exportation of specie, the value of money will increase and prices will decline. We will now trace the effect of the alteration in the value of money upon the two countries. The high prices realized in France will attract an increased exportation of commodities to that country from England. English merchants will prefer selling their commodities in France to selling them in England, because they will obtain a higher price in the former country than in the latter. For the same reasons, French merchants will prefer selling their goods in their own country to exporting them to England. In this way the exports of England to France will be increased, while her imports from France are diminished, and the position of equality between her exports and imports is restored. It may perhaps be objected to this statement that the exports of England to China are always greatly exceeded by our imports from China. The Chinese impede the importation of our merchandise, and demand silver in exchange for their exports. But it may be pointed out that we do not export gold and silver coin to China, but bullion, which is exported as an ordinary article of commerce; our large annual export of silver to China does not therefore directly affect the prices of commodities in this country, because it does not reduce the currency. The outpouring of bullion to the East has probably been very influential in checking the decline in the value of gold which it was predicted the vast discoveries in Australia and California would produce.

The meaning explained of such expressions as "balance of trade," "unfavorable exchange." In the days of the mercantile system it was thought a serious calamity to a country if a part of its exports consisted of coin or bullion. A country was in fact considered to have suffered a loss, from foreign trade, exactly equivalent to the value of the coin or bullion she exported. When a part of a nation's imports had to be paid for in gold or silver "the balance of trade" was said to be against that nation, and the exchange which she had affected was termed "unfavorable." The experience of the present century has exposed the fallacy and confusion of thought of such reasoning. Gold is now exported from the countries which produce it as an ordinary article of commerce; and the rapidity of the growth and the prosperity of Australia and California are notorious, and have been proportionate to the degree in which they have parted with their gold in exchange for the commodities produced by other countries. To consider that a country loses an amount exactly equivalent to the quantity of gold and silver she exports, is the same as thinking that everyone who buys a penny roll loses a pennyworth by the transaction.

The following chapter on Credit will explain the manner in which foreign exchanges are conducted, without involving a constant export and import of the precious metals.

QUESTIONS ON CHAPTER I. *ON FOREIGN COMMERCE*

1. What is the great advantage derived from foreign trade?
2. Give examples of this advantage.
3. What is meant by Protection, and how do protectionists justify their interference with foreign commerce?
4. What would follow if protection were withdrawn from those industries which could not survive foreign competition?
5. When a native industry would cease to exist unless it were protected from foreign competition, is loss or gain inflicted on the nation at large by protecting it?
6. What large class does the protectionist quite overlook?
7. Describe the effect produced on wages by the cheapening of any of the necessaries of life.
8. What effect is produced on the accumulation of capital by decreasing cost of production?
9. Apply the arguments of protectionists to the introduction of railway traveling.
10. Give a summary of the arguments contained in the Candle-makers' petition.
11. Under what conditions will an exchange of commodities be advantageous to both countries effecting such an exchange?
12. What must be the minimum difference in the relative value of the commodities exchanged?
13. When the difference exceeds this minimum, how are the terms of the exchange determined?

14. How does foreign commerce affect the prices of exports and imports?
15. If foreign commerce were quite unchecked, what circumstances would still cause the prices of some commodities to be different in different countries?
16. To what excess was the protective spirit carried in France before the revolution?
17. Show the manner in which the demand and supply of a foreign commodity are equalized.
18. What is "reciprocity"? Give an illustration of its impracticability in certain cases.
19. What determines the amount of profit realized by each of two countries effecting an exchange of commodities?
20. Who reaps the principal advantage from foreign trade?
21. What is the strongest case which has ever been put forward by protectionists?
22. What main advantage of free trade does this argument disregard?
23. Is this argument supported by facts?
24. Show, by an example, the manner in which protective tariffs depress industry.
25. What effect is produced on the whole population of the United States by the increasing cost of living? Quote the authority for these statements.
26. What is probably the reason why England has recognized the advantages of free trade before America?
27. Describe the tendency constantly in operation to produce an equality between the exports and imports of a country; and mention some of the circumstances which counteract this tendency.
28. Compare the effect of an export of coin with that of an export of bullion.
29. What is meant by "balance of trade" and "unfavorable exchange?"
30. Illustrate the absurdity of supposing that a country loses an amount exactly equal to the quantity of gold and silver she exports.

(*a*) In England there are taxes on tea, tobacco, and other imports; are these in any sense protective?

(*b*) If there were in a village a one-armed cobbler, who made boots rather worse and much dearer than they could be made elsewhere, and if the authorities of the village, in order to encourage native industry, levied a tax on all boots not made by him, would not this be in accordance with protectionist principles? Explain the consequences to the general well-being of the village.

(*c*) Where in America should you say the free-trade party was the strongest, in the corn-growing states of the West, or in the manufacturing districts? And give your reasons.

(*d*) Why is agriculture more profitable than manufactures in such a country as Australia?

(*e*) Trace out the results that would ensue if a country possessing rich gold fields were entirely debarred from purchasing the products of other countries.

CHAPTER TWO

CREDIT AND ITS INFLUENCE ON PRICES

DEFINITION OF CREDIT. CREDIT IS A POWER TO BORROW. IF THE CREDIT OF an individual is good, it is because there is general confidence in his ability to pay, and therefore he can borrow at a low rate of interest. If the credit of an individual is bad, he is not able to borrow except at a high rate of interest, because his ability to pay is doubted. The credit of different people in the same age and country can be accurately measured by the rate of interest which they pay for borrowing. When it is said in the City article of the *Times* that the rate of interest is "2¾ for the *best* three months' bill," it means that 2¾ percent per annum is paid for a loan by those in whose ability to pay there is perfect confidence; a higher rate of interest is paid at the same time by those whose ability to pay is less undoubted. This remark does not apply unreservedly to the credit of nations. "Ability to pay" of course produces its effect upon the credit of nations as well as upon that of individuals. The credit of Turkey and Spain is exceedingly bad. Turkish bonds for many years paid nearly 12 percent; in the autumn of 1875 the government of Turkey announced its bankruptcy by telling its creditors that only half the interest due to them would be paid in gold, and even this half was not forthcoming; some descriptions of Turkish stock are now quoted at a price, which, if they paid at all, would pay nearly £50 percent. Thus in the *Times* of July 14, 1880, the price of a Turkish bond for one hundred pounds, nominally paying 5 percent interest, was quoted at £10. 2*s*. 6*d*. Such a price as this indicates that speculators have no expectation that Turkey will resume paying interest on her debt. Spanish bonds pay about 17 percent, while English funds pay only 3¼ percent. But there is frequently a great difference between the rate of interest prevailing in two countries which does not indicate a corresponding difference in their ability to pay. It has previously been explained that the rate of interest is not only affected by the security of property and the amount of risk incurred by the lender, but also by the position of the margin of cultivation. Hence it is not fair to infer that the credit of England is better than that of America because an English government stock pays 3 percent while American government stock is issued at 5 percent. A great part of this difference is accounted for by the different position of the margin of cultivation in the two countries. In England money can be borrowed on a mortgage, that is where land is given as a security, at 4 percent, while in America money cannot be raised on a mortgage for less than 7 percent. The credit of a nation cannot therefore be accurately measured by the rate of interest which it pays for loans. Although confidence in a country's "Ability to pay" always produces its effect on the rate of interest, yet different rates of interest prevail in different countries whose financial prospects are equally sound, owing to the different position, in the scale of productiveness, of the margin of cultivation.

The expression "Credit is Capital" is meaningless. It is sometimes asserted that "Credit is Capital." A little consideration of the meaning of words shows that this expression is nonsensical. Credit has already been defined as "the power to borrow," and it has frequently been explained that capital is that part of wealth which is set aside to assist future production; it supports the laborers and furnishes the tools, materials, and shelter that their work requires. Now it is evident that a power to borrow can do none of these things. Credit will not feed and clothe laborers, nor can it furnish the implements of their industry. The power to borrow, if exerted, will procure capital, just as muscular strength will, if exerted, enable a man to carry a sack of wheat; but it is as foolish to say that credit is capital as it would be to say that a man's strength is a sack of wheat.

Banks. The real service which credit performs is that it enables an increased quantity of the wealth of a country to be used productively as capital. It encourages the productive employment of wealth. Scarcely anyone, for instance, retains a considerable sum of money in his own keeping; people keep just sufficient money to pay their daily personal expenses; all their money above this amount is generally deposited in a bank, and is there used for productive purposes. Suppose, for instance, that Mr. *A.* has an income of £1000. He deposits the whole of his yearly income in a bank, drawing it out in small sums as occasion requires. In the meantime the banker is employing a considerable part of this deposit as capital, experience having shown that a bank need never keep in the form of money more than one-third of the sums deposited with it. Mr. *A.* himself would never have been able to employ any part of his income as capital, but the banker, by accumulating a large quantity of these small capitals, is able, with advantage to all concerned, to employ two-thirds of the total amount deposited with him to assist the future production of wealth. Depositors in a bank in reality lend their money to the banker, on the condition that they shall be able to withdraw the whole or any part of their deposits at any time. In some banks depositors receive interest on their deposits, if they have been left in the bank more than a certain time. In most cases, however, the banker is considered to make a sufficient return to the depositors by taking charge of their money, and by allowing them to withdraw any part, or the whole of it, at a moment's notice. It is evident that a bank could not exist unless the credit of the banker was good. People would not place their wealth at the disposal of a man unless they had confidence in his honesty and in his ability to pay.

Joint-stock Companies. Another way in which credit enables an increased amount of the wealth that is saved to be employed productively, is by means of joint-stock companies. Such an undertaking as a railroad requires for its construction an amount of capital such as scarcely any private individual could supply. The necessary capital is therefore subscribed by thousands of individuals. The required amount is determined by the promoters of the company; it may be assumed that this amount is £1,000,000; it is accordingly arranged to raise this sum in 20,000 shares of £50 each. Any individual, therefore, who has saved £50, and who buys one of these shares, becomes what is called a shareholder in the railway; he is in fact a partner in a great commercial enterprise; this small capital of £50 is employed in assisting the future production of wealth, whereas if there had been no such things as joint-stock companies, it would probably have been consumed unproductively. It is evident that the success of a joint-stock company depends upon the credit of its promoters and directors. They have frequently not deserved the confidence reposed in their honesty, but this has nothing to do with the present subject. If their credit had not been believed to be good the companies could never have been started.

From these illustrations it is perceived that the capital of the country is practically augmented by the means of credit, because it offers great facility for the productive employment of wealth. But besides those just described there are forms of credit performing other functions, which very materially facilitate the exchange of wealth, and which produce a very great influence on the prices of commodities. The forms of credit to which we refer are bills of exchange, banknotes, cheques, and book credits.

Bills of exchange. It was said in the preceding chapter that foreign commerce did not involve a constant exchange of gold and silver money between the two countries trading with each other. It is evident that if the English merchants who purchase French goods had to send the price of these goods in money to France, great inconvenience and risk would be incurred. The necessity of the constant transit of gold and silver money is obviated in the following way. Let it be supposed that an English merchant *A.* sells £1000 worth of coal to the French merchant *B.*, and that a French merchant *C.* sells £1000 worth of wheat to the English merchant *D.* If there were no such things as bills of exchange, the result of these transactions would be a transit of £1000 in money from *B.* (in France) to *A.* (in England), and also a similar transit of £1000 in money from *D.* (in England) to *C.* (in France). Now it is evident that the same result could be attained without any transit of money at all, if *A.*, the English seller, received £1000 from *D.*, the English buyer, and *C.*, the French seller, received £1000 from *B.*, the French buyer. This result is effected in the following way. *B.*, the French merchant, sends to *A.* a written promise to pay him the £1000, and *D.*, the English merchant, sends a similar promise to pay £1000 to *C.* These written promises are called bills of exchange. *A.* has a bill for £1000 drawn on France, and *C.* has a bill for £1000 drawn on England. If they exchange these bills both debts will be discharged.

Bill discounting. Merchants do not usually effect these exchanges themselves; they are generally undertaken by a third class of individuals, called bill brokers or bill discounters. These persons undertake to buy the bills drawn on different countries. In the case just described, *A.* and *C.* would not exchange their bills; *A.* would sell his to a bill discounter in London, paying him a small sum as commission; and *C.* would sell his to a bill discounter in Paris. Thus a London bill discounter might collect £1,000,000 worth of bills drawn on France, while a French bill discounter might collect £1,000,000 worth of bills drawn on England. They would then proceed to exchange the bills. The transit of money is as entirely dispensed with as if barter were the recognized medium of exchange between the two countries.

Bills of Exchange perform many of the functions of Money, and they therefore produce an effect on General Prices. Bills of exchange are very largely used in domestic as well as in foreign commerce. It is very unusual for one merchant to pay another in money; the debt is usually discharged by means of a bill of exchange; that is, a written promise to pay at the end of a certain time. A three months' bill is a promise to pay at the end of three months, and so on. Now this bill, up to the time when it falls due, performs many of the functions of money. The person who receives it perhaps wants to make a purchase himself: we will suppose that the bill is for £1000, and that its present owner, *A.*, has received it from *B. A.* now wants to purchase £1000 worth of goods of *D.*; he obtains the goods and gives to *D.* the same bill for £1000 which *A.* had received from *B.*; at the same time *A.* endorses the bill (that is, he writes his name on the back of it) as a token that he will himself pay *D.* should *B.* fail to do so. In a similar way the bill may be used to make any number of purchases up to the time it falls due. Every time it changes hands it receives a fresh endorsement; so that at the time when it falls due the back of a bill is sometimes completely covered with endorsements. It is evident that in such a case as this a bill performs for a time the functions of money. Up to the time that it falls due it has the purchasing power of gold and silver coin. Now it has previously been explained that any circumstance which increases the amount of money circulating in a country will, if other things remain unchanged, increase the prices of commodities. The value (or exchange power) of any commodity is determined by an equalization of supply and demand. If the supply is increased, the value declines in such a degree as to equalize the demand with the augmented supply. This is true of money as of other commodities; therefore when the supply of money in a country is increased, if other things remain the same, the value of money will decline, its exchange power will diminish, and prices will rise. It is now easy to trace the influence of bills of exchange on prices. It has just been explained that a bill of exchange is, up to the time when it falls due, a substitute for money; the employment of bills of exchange, therefore, produces the same effect upon prices as if a corresponding addition had been made to the gold and silver currency. If all the business now transacted by means of bills of exchange had to be carried on with cash payments, one of two things must happen. Either a corresponding amount of money must be added to the currency, or general prices would decline. The use of bills of exchange has therefore either caused an increase in general prices, or it has prevented general prices from declining.

Banknotes. The same effect is produced on prices by other forms of credit beside bills of exchange. An issue of banknotes produces the same effect upon prices as an increase in the quantity of gold and silver coin. A banknote is simply a promise to pay; and the chief difference between a banknote and a bill of exchange is that the former is payable at any time on demand, while the latter is payable at some particular time specified on the bill. It is well known how useful a substitute for money banknotes provide; their form and portability render them particularly convenient instruments of credit. A Bank of England note is legal tender, and is in this kingdom accepted as readily as gold. The notes of provincial and private banks are not legal tender, but they are accepted with the greatest confidence by those who repose trust in the credit of the bankers who issue the notes. A Bank of England note has the same purchasing power as gold because the Bank of England is compelled by law to give gold in exchange for its notes whenever such an exchange is demanded; and everyone has perfect confidence in the solvency of the bank. All other banks are compelled by law to give either gold or Bank of England notes in exchange for their own notes. But this regulation does not compel even the most prudently managed banks to keep an equivalent in coin for all the notes they issue. It has been found that no bank need keep in cash more than a sum equal to one-third of its issue of notes. For instance, the banknote circulation of Great Britain is about £30,000,000. It may be estimated that the various banks retain in specie £10,000,000, the remaining £20,000,000 is therefore permanently added to the currency. If these £30,000,000 of notes were withdrawn, either general prices would fall or £20,000,000 in gold would have to be added to the currency. It is evident that no effect is produced on prices by an issue of banknotes if a corresponding amount of specie is at the same time withdrawn from circulation; because by such a transaction the currency is neither increased nor diminished. If, however, the issue of banknotes is increased without a corresponding withdrawal of specie, general prices will either rise or be prevented from falling.

Cheques. A cheque is a written order to a banker to pay a certain person a sum of money. If all cheques were immediately cashed by the person to whom they are payable they would produce no effect on prices. But in nearly all cases the cheque is not cashed, but is paid in by the person who receives it to his own bankers. Now let us trace the effect of this on the prices of commodities. Mr. *A.* banks with the London and Westminster Bank, he gives a cheque for £100 to Mr. *B.,* who banks with the Imperial Bank. This cheque is a written order to the directors of the London and Westminster Bank to pay £100 to Mr. *B.* Mr. *B.* does not take this cheque to the London and Westminster Bank to get it cashed, but he pays it in to his account at the Imperial Bank. In the course of the same day Mr. *C.,* who banks with the Imperial Bank, gives a cheque for £100 to Mr. *D.,* who banks with the London and Westminster Bank, and Mr. *D.* pays in the cheque to his account. At the end of the day the Imperial Bank has a cheque for £100 drawn on the London and Westminster Bank, and the London and Westminster Bank has a cheque for £100 drawn on the Imperial Bank. These banks therefore exchange the cheques, and the transit of specie from one bank to another is entirely dispensed with.

The Clearinghouse. An exchange of cheques drawn on the different banks takes place daily in London at the Clearinghouse. To this place the bankers send all the cheques which have been paid in to their banks during the day, and exchange them for cheques of a corresponding value drawn on their own banks. In this way £2,000,000,000 of cheques are annually exchanged, while to effect this exchange no specie whatever is required. Formerly after the exchange of cheques all differences were settled by cash payments; but this custom is now discontinued and the differences are settled by an account kept at the Bank of England called "the account of the Clearing Bankers." The balance for or against each bank on the day's transactions is entered in this account, and thus one entry per diem suffices for each bank. If, for instance, the London and Westminster Bank holds £100,000 of cheques drawn on the London and County Bank, while the London and County holds £110,000 of cheques drawn on the London and Westminster, the difference between them would formerly have been settled by a cash payment of £10,000, by the London and Westminster Bank to the London and County Bank. Now however all differences are settled each day by one entry for each bank "in the account of the clearing bankers" at the Bank of

England. If on the total of the day's transactions with the other clearing bankers, the London and Westminster draws upon them £1000 more than they draw upon it, the London and Westminster is credited with £1000 in the account of the clearing bankers.

It is evident that by the use of cheques and by the operations of the clearinghouse the circulation of the country is virtually increased by a very large amount, for buying and selling represented by £2,000,000,000 takes place annually, by means of cheques, without the exchange of a single farthing of money. Hence if the same amount of buying and selling went on, and cheques, or some equivalent form of credit, ceased to be used, the value of money would rise and general prices would decline; because gold and silver coin would be required in a great number of transactions which are now carried on by means of cheques.

Book Credits. Book credits can be readily explained. Suppose that an ironmonger A. buys £50 worth of coals from a coal merchant B., and that B. buys £50 worth of ironmongery from A. Instead of exchanging bills of exchange or cheques for £50, A. debits B. with £50 in his ledger, and B. does the same to A. Seeing, then, that each owes the other £50, they agree to cancel each other's debt, and the use of money is thus dispensed with.

Credit influences Prices, and not the particular form which Credit assumes. In describing these different forms of credit it should be borne in mind that it is credit which influences prices, and not the particular form credit may assume. A banknote, a cheque, or a bill of exchange, is not credit, it is simply a declaration of the existence of credit. Every form of credit which dispenses with the use of money produces an effect on prices.

The purchasing power conferred by Credit. But there is another way in which the employment of credit produces temporarily very great influence on prices. Credit very greatly increases the purchasing power of everyone who employs it. If all commodities were bought and sold for money, trade would be very seriously contracted. Suppose, for instance, that a cotton spinner desired to make a large purchase of raw cotton. He might be aware that his supply of ready money was not sufficient to effect the purchase: he therefore gives a bill of exchange to the producer of the cotton, payable at the end of three or six months; if at the end of that time he is still unable to pay, he will be able, if his credit is good, to renew the bill on paying a certain percentage. It is no doubt true the purchasing power conferred by credit may be abused by people incurring liabilities which it is highly improbable they will ever be able to meet; but without credit, speculation would be nearly impossible, and consequently the number of purchases would be greatly reduced. Since therefore credit enables a great many purchases to be made which never could take place if the payments had to be made with ready money, it is evident that credit produces an increased demand for commodities. It has frequently been proved that any circumstance which increases the demand for commodities tends to increase their price. Hence credit, by increasing the purchasing power of individuals, tends to increase the price of commodities.

Credit produces the greatest Effect on the Price of those Commodities the Supply of which is limited. It is true that the price of those commodities the supply of which can be increased tends always to approximate to the cost of production; but speculative purchases are made with the greatest frequency in those commodities the supply of which is, from exceptional circumstances, expected to be curtailed. In such cases the price of the commodity is regulated in the same way as the prices of those commodities the supply of which is absolutely limited. Thus, on the eve of the Russian war in 1854, it was known that during the war the importations from Russia of tallow, hemp, etc. would be stopped. Large speculative purchases of these commodities were therefore made with a view to the rise in price which would be occasioned by the reduced supply. Every one of these speculative purchases tended of course to raise the price of Russian goods. In the year 1869 large speculative purchases of corn were made by several corn factors, because owing to the cold and wet weather in May and June it was thought that there would be a bad harvest, and that consequently corn would be dear. These speculative purchases tended to raise the price of corn; and had the expectation of the speculators been fulfilled they would have realized large fortunes. Let us see, however, what really took place. These factors gave bills of exchange for the corn they purchased, expecting, no doubt, that by the time the bills became due, they would have sold the corn again at a higher price, or that they would be able to renew the bills in hopes of realizing yet larger gains. But although the wheat crop in England was very bad, there was an exceptionally large yield in America; the price of wheat in America was extremely low, and America immediately began exporting large quantities of wheat to England; these circumstances caused the price of corn steadily to decline. Several of the speculators were unable to meet their engagements, and many large failures ensued.

A Commercial Panic. If credit can be easily obtained it is difficult to say how great its influence may be on prices. When, however, in consequence of credit having been given too freely, prices become unduly raised above cost of production, the expectations of speculators are not fulfilled, and a large number of merchants are unable to redeem their bills; a commercial panic takes place, and credit is for a time almost entirely suspended. A crisis of this kind always involves many merchants in ruin, for they are unable, owing to the suspension of credit, to renew their bills. In consequence of the panic, traders will not accept bills of exchange; banknotes and gold become for a time in great demand; prices therefore rapidly fall, possibly as much below the cost of production as they were previously above it. Hence it is seen that when the purchasing power of credit is abused, and prices are forced up far beyond their natural rate, a commercial panic is very likely to ensue, during which credit will be as difficult to obtain as it was before carelessly granted.

The Bank Charter Act of 1844. In order to prevent the abuse of credit, and, it was thought, to ensure the community against the great loss and inconvenience of commercial panics, the Bank Charter Act of 1844 was passed. The promoters of this Act evidently thought that banknotes were the most important of all the instruments of credit, and that it was by their means that the purchasing power of speculators was increased. The Act accordingly was devised with the view of restricting the circulation of notes. The framers of the Act considered that every bank ought to have an equivalent either in bullion or in property for its issue of notes. Thus the funds, and other property possessed by the Bank of England, were estimated to be worth £15,000,000. The Act therefore decreed that if the note circulation of the Bank of England exceeded £15,000,000, the Governors of the Bank should be compelled to keep an equivalent to the excess, either in coin or bullion. Thus if the note circulation of the Bank of England is £16,000,000, the Governors of the Bank are obliged to retain in their coffers £1,000,000 of gold. The Bank Charter Act also prevented other banks from increasing their issue of notes, and provided that no bank established after the passing of the Act should be allowed to issue notes. Now it is a curious fact that for many years commercial panics took place at regular intervals with remarkable punctuality. They occurred about every nine years; and though the Bank Charter Act was devised with the express purpose of preventing panics, they did not for many years after the passing of the Act deviate from their regularity. The Act was passed in 1844; and panics occurred in 1848, 1857, and in 1866. Insofar, then, as the Act was intended to prevent commercial panics it must be considered a failure; the causes of which may now be traced. During the time of prosperous trade and good credit the purchasing power of merchants and speculators is in no degree restricted by the operation of the Bank Charter Act. The large speculative purchases which tend so powerfully to raise prices are not made by means of banknotes, but by bills of exchange. Banknotes are as difficult to get as money, because they can at any moment be changed for money. Hence during times of commercial security and tranquility the Act is inoperative; it remains to be seen what its effect is during the panics, which it is powerless to prevent. During a panic there is a general desire to discount bills, money is at a premium; everyone who owns bills of exchange is desirous of changing them for money, on account of the insecurity which prevails. Hence during a panic the Bank is urged to discount an unusually large number of bills, and the rate of discount rapidly rises. Now the Bank Charter Act effectually restricts the amount of accommodation the Bank is able to give, for it provides that the Bank shall purchase an equivalent in bullion for all notes which it issues over a certain amount. When therefore this sum is reached the issue of notes is stopped, because it would be no longer profitable to the Bank to continue it. Hence the rate of discount is still further augmented because the supply of credit is artificially restricted. No other instrument of credit is able at such a crisis to produce the same effect as banknotes; people will not accept bills of exchange because the public confidence is disturbed, and a general feeling of insecurity prevails. Bank of England notes are, on the contrary, as readily accepted as gold, because they can always be exchanged for gold on demand at the Bank. It is therefore seen that the Bank Charter Act does not prevent reckless speculation and an undue extension of credit during periods of commercial tranquility; and when public confidence is shaken and a commercial panic takes place, the Act absolutely limits the amount of accommodation the Bank can afford. This fact has been so far recognized by legislators and the Bank authorities, that the Act has been temporarily suspended during each of the three panics that have occurred since the passing of the Act. On every occasion after the suspension of the Act the rate of discount has rapidly subsided; the suspension of the Act served in a great measure to allay the excitement which prevailed, because it was thought that after the suspension there would be no scarcity of money. In 1857 and in 1866 about £1,000,000 extra notes were issued by the Bank; nearly all of these were returned to the Bank in a few days, and the currency gradually returned to its normal condition. The uncertainty whether the Act will be suspended or not, adds another element of excitement to the general frenzy that prevails during a panic. The merchants and speculators know that the Act will probably be temporarily suspended during the panic, but the exact day and hour of the suspension are of course unknown. The time at which this takes place may make all the difference to a speculator between solvency and ruin.

The Suspension of the Act protects solvent Merchants without sparing those who have speculated rashly. It is, however, to be observed that the suspension of the Act does not retard the ruin of those who speculate rashly, and who are really insolvent; the directors of the Bank, in their own interest, take care to discount only good bills, and they are more cautious in this respect during a panic than they are at any other time. The suspension of the Act saves those from failure who are really solvent and wealthy, but who conduct their business on the justifiable expectation that they will be able to renew and discount bills: the sudden contraction of credit which accompanies a panic often involves such persons in ruin through no fault of their own. Although the Bank Charter Act has been powerless to prevent panics, and although it appears occasionally to aggravate their intensity, there is a service rendered by this Act which goes far to outweigh any inconveniences it may temporarily produce. Bank of England notes are in this country legal tender; that is to say, that all debts may be legally discharged in Bank of England notes. A creditor can legally claim to be paid either in coin or in Bank of England notes; he is not compelled to accept the notes of any other bank. The Bank of England is bound by law to give gold, on demand, in exchange for its own notes: and the Bank Charter Act gives an absolute guarantee to the public that the Bank shall always be able to fulfil this condition. By the regulations of this Act, after the Bank has issued £15,000,000 of notes, it can issue no more without placing in the coffers of the bank an amount of coin or bullion corresponding in value to the sum which the notes represent. The Act therefore ensures that there shall be no inflation of the currency through an excessive issue of Bank of England notes, and in this way it provides a guarantee for the convertibility of the notes of the Bank. The whole of the credit system of this country centers in the Bank of England. Every country banker keeps an account with a London banker, and all the London bankers keep accounts at the Bank of England. The importance, therefore, of giving a legal guarantee for the convertibility of Bank of England notes can hardly be exaggerated.

Convertible and Inconvertible Paper Currency. It has frequently been stated that in this country banknotes can always be exchanged for gold. It is the law of the country that a private bank should always give gold or Bank of England notes, on demand, in exchange for its own notes; and that the Bank of England should always give gold, on demand, in exchange for its notes. This regulation makes ours what is called a "convertible paper currency"; that is to say, it can be exchanged at any time for gold. In some other countries, Italy for instance, there is an "inconvertible paper currency"; that is to say, the notes are not convertible into money on demand, and the paper currency is depreciated, that is, a paper *lire* is worth less than a silver *lire*. In exchange for a sovereign the English traveler in Italy gets 25 *lire* in silver, or 27 *lire* 40 centimes in paper. No injustice is done to anyone by an issue of inconvertible notes if they are not made legal tender, because then no one need accept them who would rather be paid in gold. There are, however, always many dangers connected with the use of inconvertible notes. There is, practically, no limit to their issue, and such enormous sums may be by their means added to the currency as seriously to disturb the finances of the country, and to undermine the credit of the Government. The extraordinarily large issue of these inconvertible notes in America during the war caused a disparity in value between the gold and the notes, because it was not confidently believed that the Government would be able to redeem the notes. Gold was at a premium, and the notes, or greenbacks as they are called, were at a discount. This disparity rapidly diminished as the United States began to recover from the effects of the Civil War; and it has now entirely ceased because by resuming specie payments the paper money of the United States has become a convertible currency. Once during the Civil War £100 in gold exchanged for £180 in notes. In Jan. 1870 £100 in gold exchanged for £120 of notes, and in July 1871 £100 in gold exchanged for £112 of notes; and it remained at about this figure until shortly before the resumption of specie payments. The large issue of these notes in America had a very great influence in raising prices in that country. The loss of credit sustained by the American Government by too large an issue of inconvertible notes produced a disparity in value between gold and greenbacks, and this circumstance brought into existence a class of speculators whose operations were most detrimental to the interests of legitimate industry. These people speculated in gold, that is, they treated gold as an ordinary article of commerce, buying up large quantities of it in hopes of increasing its value.

The Gold Ring of New York. The speculations of the Gold Ring of New York became famous all over the world in the autumn of 1869. The members of the Gold Ring conspired together to buy up all the gold in the country, and all the gold cheques. (The latter are instruments of credit in the form of cheques, and payable in gold coin, not in greenbacks.) These large purchases of gold began to produce effect in September 1869, when the members of the Ring held nearly all the gold in New York; the amount owed to them being estimated at 100,000,000 dollars. As the gold owing to them was paid in, they stored it away, and the value of gold began rapidly to advance. The gold speculators thought that they would be able to force up the value of gold 100 percent. The only thing which they feared would mar their designs was a sale of gold by the Government. Against this contingency they endeavored in vain to protect themselves; they therefore were obliged to be content with the hope that they would raise the price of gold so quickly, that there would not be time for the Government to suspect the plot. Their expectations were very nearly realized. In one morning before 12 o'clock the value of gold rose from 130 to 160, At 12 o'clock the Secretary of the Treasury ordered a sale of four millions of Government gold; the plot of the Ring was frustrated, and in eight minutes the value of gold fell 12½ percent. At 12 o'clock it was at 160, and at eight minutes past 12 it was at 140; in nineteen minutes more the premium was only 33 (*Fraser's Magazine,* Jan. 1870). It is not necessary to dwell upon the injury inflicted upon legitimate industry by the possibility of such occurrences as that just described. It casts a hazardous uncertainty over the transactions of every merchant: and all business partakes more or less of the nature of gambling.

The influence of Credit on General Prices is beneficial. Where credit is kept within legitimate bounds, there is no doubt that its influence on prices is beneficial to the general interests of the community. For the use of credit tends to prevent those fluctuations in general prices which are always so disastrous to production, owing to the uncertainty which they cast over commercial transactions. The manner in which credit tends to prevent fluctuations in general prices may be perhaps best described by tracing the operation in this direction of bills of exchange. It has often been explained that the more buying and selling there is, the more money is required; and, if no more money or no substitute for money is forthcoming, prices must decline. With every increase of buying and selling a direct tendency is exerted to increase the number of bills of exchange. If a merchant doubles his buying and selling, he will be sure to give and receive a far larger number of bills of exchange. Hence every increase in commerce produces spontaneously an increased use of credit. A corresponding influence is exerted when trade declines, for when buying and selling are restricted, a smaller number of bills of exchange is employed. If it were not for the use of credit every fresh development of commerce would produce a decrease in general prices, and prices would rise during periods of stagnation in trade. The elasticity of credit thus has a very beneficial influence in preventing great fluctuations in general prices, although in isolated cases the use of credit sometimes produces the most rapid variations in the price of a commodity.

The Direct Economy of a Paper Currency. There is one more advantage derived from the use of credit, which has not been noticed. It has been pointed out that the paper currency of any country forms a more or less complete substitute for money. If banknotes, cheques, and bills of exchange ceased to be used, a much larger quantity of gold and silver coin would be required. Hence there is a direct economy in the employment of these instruments of credit, because a comparatively worthless substance like paper is used as a substitute for the highly valuable commodities, gold and silver. The material of which a Bank of England note for £1000 is composed does not cost as much as a farthing; its intrinsic value is inappreciably small, but owing to the purchasing power which credit confers upon it, it is as useful to its owner as 1000 sovereigns.

QUESTIONS ON CHAPTER II. *CREDIT, AND ITS INFLUENCE ON PRICES*

1. What is Credit?
2. What is the test of the credit of an individual or of a nation?
3. What other circumstance besides "ability to pay" produces different rates of interest in different countries?
4. Why is it foolish to assert that credit is capital?
5. Explain the nature of the service which credit renders to the production of wealth.
6. How do banks promote the productive employment of wealth?
7. How do joint-stock companies promote the productive employment of wealth?
8. Show that the existence of banks and joint-stock companies depends upon credit.
9. What are bills of exchange, and in what way do they facilitate the exchange of wealth?
10. What is meant by discounting a bill?
11. Explain the manner in which a bill performs the functions of money.
12. What is endorsing a bill?
13. What effect does credit, in the form of bills of exchange, produce upon prices?
14. Why does credit tend to raise the prices of commodities?
15. What would be the consequence, did bills of exchange or some similar instruments of credit cease to be used?
16. What is a banknote?
17. Wherein does a banknote differ from a bill of exchange?
18. Why have Bank of England notes the same purchasing power as gold?
19. How do banknotes influence prices?
20. What are cheques, and how do they provide a substitute for money?
21. What is the Clearinghouse?
22. State the annual value of the cheques exchanged in the Clearinghouse.
23. What are book credits, and how do they obviate the exchange of coin?

24. How does credit increase the purchasing power of individuals?
25. What effect has this increased purchasing power on prices?
26. On the price of what class of commodities does credit produce the greatest effect?
27. What is the cause of commercial panics?
28. What effect do they produce on credit?
29. What was the object of the Bank Charter Act?
30. What are the provisions of the Act?
31. Has the Act been successful in preventing panics?
32. Describe the regularity with which panics recur, and name the years in which they have taken place since the passing of the Act.
33. Explain why the Act does not restrict the purchasing power of speculators.
34. What is the real effect of the Act?
35. Why, during a panic, would Bank of England notes be accepted, when all other instruments of credit are refused?
36. How often and on what occasions has the Bank Charter Act been suspended?
37. What has been the effect of the suspension of the Act?
38. Name the great service guaranteed by the Act.
39. What is meant by a convertible and an inconvertible paper currency?
40. What are the dangers connected with an issue of inconvertible notes?
41. Describe the famous operations of the New York Gold Ring.
42. Explain the manner in which credit tends to prevent fluctuation in general prices.
43. How is a direct economy involved in the use of paper money?
    (*a*) Does a man who forges a banknote add to the wealth of the country?
    (*b*) Am I wicked for having £1000 at my banker's and not using it?
    (*c*) Would a banker make himself poorer if he burnt one of his own £1000 notes?
    (*d*) Can a banker make himself rich by issuing notes?
    (*e*) Can anyone make himself rich by writing cheques?

CHAPTER THREE

On Taxation

THE NECESSITY OF TAXATION. THE LEGITIMATE FUNCTIONS OF government are generally admitted to be the protection of life and property, and the maintenance of the equal freedom of all. These functions cannot be performed without incurring a considerable expense. To meet this expense taxation is necessary; great interest has always been felt in the questions how taxes should be levied and on what classes they should fall. It has of late years been rightly considered that everyone who benefits by the protection which such institutions as a standing army and the constabulary afford, should contribute to defray the expense which their maintenance necessarily incurs. In feudal times this principle was not recognized. There is no doubt that one of the immediate causes of the French Revolution was the immunity from taxation enjoyed by the French nobles and clergy. The whole weight of taxation was thus thrust on the poorer classes, who were not allowed any voice in the management of the national finances. At the present time the principles of justice are not so grossly violated; no class is allowed to enjoy immunity from taxation, but rates and taxes are now levied from all classes indiscriminately; no exemption from taxation is permitted to anyone on the ground that he does not approve of the object to which the money raised by taxation is devoted. For instance, a part of the national revenue of this country is expended in providing secret service money, and in paying large salaries and pensions to those who possess sinecure offices. However strongly individuals may object to this expenditure of public money, they are obliged to contribute as much to the revenue as if they most warmly approved it. There is practically no injustice in this; at least so far as regards those persons who possess the privilege of Parliamentary representation.

Adam Smith's Four Canons of Taxation. In Adam Smith's *Wealth of Nations* he laid down four canons of taxation, the due observance of which secures minimum hardship to the taxpayer and maximum revenue to the state. These four canons are too long to be here transcribed in full. The following is a summary of them:

First. Every subject ought to contribute to the revenue a sum proportionate to the income which he enjoys under the protection of the State.

Second. Taxes ought to be certain, not arbitrary. The time of payment, the manner of payment, the quantity to be paid, ought to be clear and plain to the contributor and to every other person.

Third. Every tax ought to be levied at the time and in the manner in which it is most convenient for the contributor to pay it.

Fourth. Every tax ought to be so contributed as both to take out and keep out of the pockets of the people as little as possible over and above what it brings into the public treasury of the State.

The application of the First Canon. The first of these canons cannot be observed in respect to each individual tax. It would be impossible to adjust each tax in proportion to the means of the taxpayer, or his ability to pay. For instance, a family of six persons who had only just sufficient income to live on, would probably consume as much, or even more tea than a wealthy family of half the size. The poorer family therefore pays much more duty on tea in proportion to its income than the wealthy family. It is obviously impossible for any government to provide against cases of this sort. If it were attempted, thousands of government officials would have to be employed in the inspection and investigation of special cases, and probably the whole amount raised by the tax would be consumed in paying the salaries of these officials. Thus in attempting to carry out

Adam Smith's first canon, the government would be led into a flagrant violation of his fourth canon. The equality of taxation is best preserved, not by attention to one particular tax, but by endeavoring to make the aggregate amount of taxation paid by different classes of persons proportionate to the incomes they enjoy. Thus in the case just noticed though the poor family pays more duty on tea, in proportion to its income, than the rich family, it would pay less as income tax, and less in duty on all articles of luxury, such as wine and spirits. In this way a rough kind of equality is preserved.

The application of the Second Canon. Adam Smith's second rule, that taxes ought to be certain and not arbitrary, is of very great importance. When traders are uncertain how much duty they will have to pay on the commodities in which they deal, an air of uncertainty and speculation is thrown over commercial transactions; men depend more on their luck than on their sagacity and prudence, and trade becomes a gigantic system of gambling. The violation of this rule is the great disadvantage of *ad valorem* duties on imported commodities in comparison with duties of a fixed money value.

The Third Canon. The third rule is obviously necessary to ensure the minimum of hardship to the taxpayer. If taxes are levied at a time which is unnecessarily inconvenient to the taxpayer, an injury is inflicted on him without any compensating benefit to the community at large. All taxes on commodities are really paid by the consumer, because they form part of cost of production. The consumer therefore pays the tax at a time when it is convenient to him to do so, viz. when he makes the purchase: if it were an inconvenient time for him to pay the tax he could abstain from purchasing the commodity. Taxes on commodities are, however, in the first place paid by the seller. Thus if a man buys a pound of tea, a part of the price is the duty which is levied by the State on this commodity. The retail trader has already paid the duty when he purchased the tea. If he had had to pay for it in ready money it might have been an extremely inconvenient time for him to pay the tax, but he probably effected the purchase with a bill of exchange for three or six months; at the end of this time he will have sold the tea to his customers, and thus have obtained the means to redeem his bill. "A tax on the rent of land, or of houses, payable at the same time at which such rents are usually paid, is levied at a time when it is most likely to be convenient for the contributor to pay; or when he is most likely to have wherewithal to pay" (Adam Smith).

The Fourth Canon. The utility of Bonding Houses. The fourth rule is intimately connected with the third. If a tax is levied at a time when it is inconvenient for the contributor to pay, it is nearly sure to take much more from the pockets of the taxpayer than it yields to the revenue of the State. When inconvenience of paying a particular tax is obviated by special arrangement, the discrepancy between the amount yielded to the State and that taken from the taxpayer is diminished. Thus if a merchant who imports taxed commodities does not wish to sell them immediately, he can place them in a bonding house. As long as they remain in bond he pays no duty upon them. They can remain in bond until they are sold; the merchant therefore pays the duty at a most convenient time to himself, viz. at the time that he sells the commodities and is in receipt of their price. Let us see what influence is thus produced on the price of commodities. Suppose a wine merchant imports £1000 worth of wine, and that the duty on the wine is £500. He places the wine in a bonding house, where it remains six months, when it is sold. If the wine merchant makes a profit of 20 percent per annum on his capital this wine will be sold for £1600. This will be composed of the following items:

Original cost of wine	£1000
10 percent six months' profit on wine merchant's outlay	£100
Duty on the wine	£500
	£1600

Now if the wine merchant had had to pay the duty directly the wine arrived in the dock, its price, after six months, would be £1650 instead of £1600; because the merchant would have employed £500 more capital on which he would expect to receive interest at the rate of 20 percent per annum. The items of the price of the wine will then be as follows:

Price of wine, including duty	£1500
Wine merchant's profit of £10 percent for the six months on this outlay	£150
	£1650

The purchaser of the wine would therefore pay in consequence of the duty £50 more than ever reaches the revenue of the State.[1]

Taxes on Raw Materials. In accordance with Adam Smith's fourth rule, taxes on commodities should not be levied on the raw material, but on the manufactured goods. If, for instance, it were considered desirable to put a tax on cotton, the tax should not be levied on raw cotton, but on the manufactured material. Cotton in the process of manufacture passes through the hands of a considerable number of traders. If the tax is levied on the raw material, each one of these different traders has to pay the tax, and the interest on the outlay of him of whom the purchase is made. If $A.$, the importer, pays £1000 in duty on cotton, he expects when he sells it to $B.$ to have the ordinary rate of profit, say £10 percent, on this outlay. $B.$ therefore pays £1100 in consequence of the duty, and when he sells it to $C.$ he expects 10 percent interest on this £1100; $C.$ therefore pays £1210. Every time the material changes hands the amount paid in consequence of the duty increases at compound interest, until when it reaches the consumer, who really bears the burden of the tax, the amount added to the price of the commodity in consequence of the tax may be double the sum which is received by the State treasury. In order, therefore, to carry out Adam Smith's fourth rule commodities ought to be taxed as nearly as possible at the time when they are purchased for consumption; for the burden of the tax being really borne by the consumer, he ought not to be made to pay the interest on the additional outlay (caused by the tax) of the numerous merchants through whose hands a commodity passes in process of manufacture. The proposal contained in Mr. Gladstone's budget of 1880 to abolish the malt tax and substitute for it a tax on beer, was quite in accordance with Adam Smith's fourth Canon.

Direct Taxation on Commodities is impracticable. Some have thought that the interest of the consumer would be best protected if the taxes on commodities were collected in the shops where they are sold. For instance, that if a woman went into a shop to buy a pound of tea, the shopkeeper should say the price of the tea is 2*s*. 6*d*., and the tax is 6*d*. But this plan, in attempting to carry out Adam Smith's fourth rule, would inevitably violate it more completely than it is violated by the present system. Armies of Government officials, whose salaries would probably equal, if not exceed the whole amount yielded by the tax, would have to be constantly employed in looking over shopkeepers' books, and in ascertaining that the right amount of duty had been handed over by the shopkeepers to the state. Even this great expenditure would probably be powerless to prevent some of the shopkeepers evading the yielding up of the duty. To ensure economical collection a tax should be levied at a time when the commodity is not dispersed among a large number of retail tradesmen, but when it is amassed in large quantities in the warehouse of a wholesale merchant. The means of evading the tax are in this way diminished.

The cost of collecting Taxes should be as far as possible reduced. There is no doubt that Adam Smith's fourth rule might be much more strictly observed if strenuous efforts were made to reduce the cost of collection of some of the taxes. Take, for instance, the cost of collecting the customs' revenue. A return has been issued by a private society showing the gross amount, cost of collection, and net produce of the customs' revenue in 1868; and the gross amount, expense, and net yield of each customhouse. This return shows, that although the net gain to the country from the customs' revenue is very considerable, yet "out of the 132 customhouses, sixty-six, or exactly one-half, are a loss to the country." "Adding the extra expenses not separately allotted by Government, over one hundred out of the 132 customhouses are a loss to the country." A table of the customhouses which are a loss to the country affords many striking instances of the violation of Adam Smith's fourth rule. The following are a few of the most striking cases:

Town.	Total cost of collection.	Revenue collected in 1868	Loss to the country.
Aberystwith	£1913	£73	£1840
Borrowstoness	1586	401	1185
Kirkwall	2076		2076
Lerwick	1376		1376
Milford	3313	147	3166
Rye	1236	5	1231
Scilly	1143	1	1142

The incidence of Taxation. Direct and Indirect Taxation.
Before proceeding to an explanation of the nature of special taxes, such as the income tax and the land tax, it will be well to point out what is meant by the incidence of taxation, and the difference between direct and indirect taxation. "A direct tax is one which is demanded from the very persons who, it is intended or desired, should pay it. Indirect taxes are those which are demanded from one person in the expectation and intention that he shall indemnify himself at the expense of another: such as the excise or customs" (*Principles of Pol. E.* Vol. II p. 404). The incidence of taxation is borne by the person out of whose pocket the tax really comes. For instance, the incidence of taxes on commodities is borne by the consumer, because although the tax is, in the first place, paid by the manufacturers or importers, it increases the price of the commodity, and is finally paid by the consumer. The incidence of poor rates (as far as agricultural land is concerned) is borne entirely by landowners, for though the rates are levied on the farmer, they reduce the rent of the landlord. If the landlord paid the poor rates the farmer would pay more rent. Though generally paid by the farmers, the poor rates in reality come out of the landlords' pockets. The incidence of all assessed taxes such

as the dog tax, the tax on carriages, livery servants, and hair powder, and, in most instances, the income tax, is upon the person on whom the tax is in the first place levied. A tax is called indirect when it is levied on one person, while the incidence of the tax is on another. The incidence of a direct tax is upon the same person upon whom the tax is in the first place levied. Taxes on commodities are therefore indirect, while assessed taxes, and, generally speaking, the income tax are direct.

The Income Tax. The income tax is an impost of so much in the pound levied on all incomes over £150 per annum. For instance, if the income tax is 6*d*. in the pound, everyone in receipt of an income of £1000 a year has to contribute a thousand sixpences or £25 to the State as income tax. When this tax was first established it was considered a temporary expedient, and it was confidently believed that the tax would soon be remitted. Although it constantly varies in amount the tax has never been remitted, and after the experience gained in the general election of 1874, when its remission was advocated by the leader of one of the great political parties, it does not appear that there is a general desire in the country to repeal the income tax. The question whether the income tax should be considered as a permanent or a temporary impost is of great importance in deciding whether the tax is economically justifiable. The question whether the same amount of income tax should be levied on temporary and on permanent incomes has given rise to much discussion. It may be shown that the argument entirely turns on the point, whether the income tax is permanent and fixed in amount, or whether it is temporary and variable. If it is permanent and fixed, the same amount should be levied from all incomes whether temporary or otherwise. If the tax is only imposed for a short time, with the view of remitting it as soon as possible, temporary incomes ought to be taxed at a lower rate than permanent incomes. Let us take an instance of the first case, viz. where the income tax is permanent and fixed in amount. Mr. *A.* is in receipt of an income of £1000 a year arising from landed property; Mr. *B.* derives an income of £1000 from his profession as a doctor. It is urged by some that it is very hard to tax the temporary income of Mr. B. at the same rate as the permanent income of Mr. A. It is said that Mr. B.'s income is derived entirely by his own exertions, and that it will cease at his death. This plea points out the very reason why both incomes should be taxed at the same rate. Supposing the income tax to be fixed and permanent, the income which Mr. A. derives from his landed property will go on being taxed forever; whereas Mr. B.'s income, which is derived from a temporary source, will cease to be taxed when it ceases to exist, at Mr. B.'s death. The case may be further elucidated by another example. Suppose that three people each have £20,000 left them. A. invests his £20,000 in landed property, which brings him in £500 a year; B. purchases an annuity which ensures him £1500 a year for the rest of his life; while C. purchases an annuity of £2500 a year, to last for 10 years. Now all these incomes are derived from an exactly equal amount of capital. The one income is permanent, the second depends on the life of an individual, and the third will cease at the end of a certain term of years. Supposing the income tax to be permanent and fixed, there is no reason why A.'s income should be taxed at a higher rate than B.'s or C.'s. If the income tax is 3d. in the pound A.'s income will pay £6. 5s. a year as income tax forever, B.'s will pay £18. 15s. a year for the rest of his life; and C.'s will pay £31. 5s. a year for 10 years. The value of these sums when capitalized is equal; and if A., B., and C. wished to pay such a sum down as would exonerate their incomes from further payment of income tax, each would have to pay the same amount. If however the income tax were only a temporary impost, it would be unjust to tax temporary and permanent incomes at the same rate. Suppose for instance that an income tax of 3d. in the pound were imposed for 10 years. In the case above described, C. would in 10 years pay as much income tax as A. would if the tax were continued forever. The same inequality, though in a minor degree, takes place when the income tax varies in amount.

If the Income tax is permanent in duration and fixed in amount, temporary and permanent incomes should be taxed at the same rate. Thus it may be laid down as a general rule that when the income tax is permanent and fixed in amount, all incomes, whether temporary or otherwise, should be taxed at the same rate; if however the income tax is temporary in its duration, and uncertain in amount, permanent incomes should be taxed at a higher rate than temporary incomes. In the case of the income tax being temporary in its duration, perfect equality could only be obtained by capitalizing all incomes and annually deducting by means of the income tax so much percent of their capitalized value. But this arrangement would be found quite impracticable, for in the case of temporary incomes endless difficulty and expense would follow an attempt to capitalize them. Government officials would have to examine all the receivers of temporary incomes and fix the amount of the income tax which they had to pay, in accordance with their age and the state of their health. For instance, two half-pay officers of the same age, each receiving £200 a year, might have to be taxed at different rates, because the one being much healthier than the other, would be likely to live longer, and the capitalized value of his income would therefore be greater than that of the other. If therefore an attempt were made to adjust the income tax according to the capitalized value of each income, the expense of collecting the tax would absorb an undue proportion of the sum which it yields to the treasury. This is an example of the assertion previously made, that legislators should strive to produce a general equality in the gross amount of taxation, and not endeavor to adjust each particular tax in accordance with the ability of the contributor to pay.

The Income Tax presses more heavily on the possessors of small incomes than on the possessors of large incomes. The income tax has been objected to on the ground that it presses much more severely on the possessor of a very small income than on the possessor of a large income. Thus if the income tax were 6*d.* in the pound, and if it were levied on all incomes, the possessor of an income of £100 would have to pay £2. 10*s.* a year; the possessor of an income of £10,000 would have to pay £250 a year. Now it may be urged that £100 a year is only barely sufficient to provide the necessaries of life; especially if it is assumed that the possessor of such an income has an average-sized family depending upon him. £2. 10*s.*

cannot be deducted from this income without depriving its possessor or those depending on him of sufficient food, clothing, shelter and warmth to ensure health and the absence of bodily suffering. To deduct £250 annually from an income of £10,000 inflicts no hardship on the possessor of this income; it may only reduce in some measure his consumption of luxuries. In order to provide a remedy for this inequality, it was suggested by Bentham that a certain minimum of income, sufficient to provide the necessaries of life, should be left untaxed; and that this amount should be deducted from all incomes, the remainder only to be taxed. For instance, if this minimum were fixed at £100, no income of this amount and under should be taxed at all; an income of £120 should lie taxed only on £20; while an income of £1000 should be taxed only on £900. By this means "each would then pay a certain fixed proportion of his superfluities." At the present time this scheme has not been carried into practice. The following modification of it is adopted: No income of less than £150 is taxed, and £120 is deducted from all incomes between £150 and £400. For instance, an income of £200 is only taxed on £80. This plan is not so accurately just as that proposed by Bentham. For instance, an income of £150 would not be taxed at all, while an income of £155 would be taxed on £35; an income of £400 would be taxed on £280, while an income of £405 would be taxed on its whole amount. The plan which has been adopted, has, however, the great practical advantage, that it is of much easier application than the scheme recommended by Bentham.

The Income tax is usually a direct tax; it is sometimes indirect. At first sight it appears that the income tax is always a direct tax, but it may be shown that there are cases in which income tax is an indirect tax. When the income tax is paid out of savings which would not otherwise be productively employed, it is a direct tax, because it is really borne by the person who pays the tax; but when the income tax is paid out of capital it is an indirect tax, for it then falls partly on the laborers who would have been maintained by the capital used to pay the tax. For example, suppose that a manufacturer has to pay £1000 a year as income tax, and that if this impost were not placed upon him he would use this sum in employing a larger number of laborers; it is evident, in such a case as this, that the tax falls partly on the laboring classes, because it reduces the wages fund, and therefore tends to lower the rate of wages. If, however, the manufacturer pays this £1000, not out of capital, but by reducing his consumption of luxuries, then the income tax is a direct tax, and comes out of the pocket of the person who pays it. The income tax is a severe burden upon industry if it is paid out of capital. It should never be imposed except in such countries as England, where there is an abundance of capital for carrying out commercial enterprises, and where consequently the income tax does not retard the production of wealth.

Some dishonest people have the power to evade paying the full amount of the Income Tax. It is urged as an objection to the income tax that some dishonest people have opportunities of avoiding it by declaring their incomes to be smaller than they really are. The consideration whether any particular tax affects injuriously the morality of the people is one which no statesman is justified in neglecting. At the same time there is perhaps scarcely sufficient evidence to prove that the income tax is the cause of the dishonesty of the people who evade it. It no doubt affords them an opportunity of being dishonest, but they would not avail themselves of the opportunity unless they were disposed to do so. Under the present condition of things it can hardly therefore be considered a valid objection to the income tax that it affords some dishonest people an opportunity of cheating the government and the rest of the taxpayers.

Taxes on commodities should be levied on luxuries rather than on necessaries. Some of the remarks just made on the subject of the income tax throw some light on the consideration of taxes on commodities. It was shown that the income tax ought not to be levied on those incomes which are sufficient only to procure the necessaries of life. It was laid down as a rule that each ought to contribute to the imperial exchequer a certain proportion of his superfluities. It therefore appears that taxes on commodities ought, in accordance with this rule, to be confined to luxuries, and should not be levied on the necessaries of life. If it be admitted that those persons ought to be as far as possible relieved from taxation whose incomes are sufficient only to provide them with necessaries, it is clear that the cost of these necessaries ought not to be increased by taxation. On the other hand there is no reason why the luxuries consumed by the poorer classes of the community, such as beer, spirits, and tobacco, should not be taxed. If a man's income be sufficient to procure luxuries, he ought not to be entirely relieved from taxation on the ground of poverty; he ought to contribute to the State a certain proportion of his superfluities.

Taxes on land fall on the owner of the land, and not on the cultivator. It may be generally stated that all taxes which are levied on land, such as the land tax, the tithe, and the poor rate, really fall on the owner of the land, and not on the cultivator. If these charges are in the first instance paid by the cultivating tenant, he pays so much less rent. If he ceases to pay the tax his rent is increased. A reduction of the poor rate on land, therefore, is no permanent or direct benefit to the tenant; at the first opportunity his rent will be raised by a sum corresponding to the amount of taxation of which he has been relieved.

The land tax is really Rent. The land tax is in this country constantly becoming smaller in proportion to the value of land; its pecuniary amount is fixed, and it does not therefore advance with the increasing value of agricultural produce. The land tax, whether small or great in amount, partakes of the nature of a rent paid by the owner of land to the State, and it thus recognizes, in some degree, the proprietary rights of the State. In a great part of India the land is owned by the government, and therefore the land tax is rent, paid direct by the cultivating tenants to the State. These tenants, instead of holding under private owners, hold under the State, and the rent which they pay is called land tax. The economic perfection of this system of tenure may be readily perceived. It has been shown that as population increases, the value of land, owing to no exertions on the part of the owner or cultivator, increases, on account of the increased value of agricultural produce. In a system of land tenure, where land is owned by private individuals, all this additional value is shared by a few persons who happen to be the owners of land. In a system of land tenure, where the land is owned by the State, this additional value is shared by the whole nation, and may be devoted to the relief of taxation. A great part of that wealth which is taken out of the pockets of the people by the increased price of food, is returned to them in the shape of the larger rents which are paid into the national exchequer. The land revenue of India amounts to £22,000,000 annually. The payment of this large amount is a burden to no one; if it were not paid to the State it would be paid to landlords. No one is injured by the payment of this sum; on the contrary, a much larger amount of taxation would have to be levied if the land were owned by private individuals; for in this case the national revenue would be diminished by £22,000,000 annually, and this deficiency would have to be supplied by increased taxation. It is clear that the land tax should never exceed the economic rent; i.e., the surplus which remains after defraying all the expenses of cultivation, including the average rate of profit on the capital of the cultivator. It has been shown that this surplus is equal to the difference in value between the land in question and the worst land in cultivation which pays no rent. If the land tax exceed the economic rent, the cultivation of the worst land, which formerly paid no rent, will cease to be profitable, and it will consequently fall out of cultivation. The supply of food will be diminished and prices will rise. The excessive land tax will lead to increasing the supply of food by means of foreign importations. When therefore the land tax exceeds the economic rent, a double tendency is exerted to throw land out of cultivation, and consequently the area from which the tax is collected is decreased.

Tithes are a charge on Landed Property. Tithes are a charge on landed property; they were originally imposed for the maintenance of religious establishments. As the name implies, they formerly amounted to one-tenth of the produce. The appropriation of tithes for religious purposes was abolished in the time of the Reformation, and tithes are now very frequently owned by private individuals who have no share in the cultivation, management, or possession of the land. The difficulty of assessing the tithe led to the passing, in 1837, of the Tithe Commutation Act; by which the amount of tithe paid is regulated according to the average price of corn during the previous seven years. By this arrangement the tithe proprietor was excluded from benefiting by the increased productiveness of land. He would indeed be a sufferer by any circumstance which might, for example, double the yield of corn. For such an event would reduce the price of corn, and would accordingly diminish the amount of the tithe. The Tithe Commutation Act also tends to diminish the proportional value of the tithe, for reasons which were probably unforeseen by those who passed the Act in 1837. Corn can be easily imported from foreign countries. An immense quantity has since 1847 been annually imported into this country. Livestock, milk, butter, etc. cannot be so easily imported; therefore the relative value of corn, as compared with meat and dairy produce, will tend to diminish as population increases. Hence the tithe, being determined solely by the average price of corn, will not increase proportionally with the increased value of agricultural produce considered as a whole.

The Incidence of Poor Rates levied on Dwelling Houses. Without attempting to describe the social effects of the poor rates, it is desirable to give a short account of their incidence and some of their economic consequences. The poor rates are levied only on real property, such as land, trade premises, and houses. It has already been pointed out that in agricultural land poor rates are really borne by the owner of the land. It has been long a disputed point whether in the case of house property the incidence of poor rates is on the occupier or the owner. If the reduction or abolition of the poor rate increased the rent of houses by an amount exactly corresponding to the sum which was formerly levied on the same houses as poor rate, then the whole incidence of the rate is on the landlord, because the rate reduces his rent. But it must be remembered that the poor rate is levied, not only on the land on which the house is built, but on the house itself. For instance, a certain house pays £9 a year ground rent, and £60 as house rent. The poor rates levied on this house average £9 annually. The rate is levied at so much in the pound of the entire rental, and not on the ground rent only. Now it is evident that the builder of the house does not bear the rate any more than a grocer bears the duty on tea. The builder gets the average rate of profit of his trade; this profit being composed of the following elements; the current rate of interest, compensation for risk, and wages of superintendence. The poor rate does not come out of his pocket, but it increases the cost of production, just in the same way as the duty on wine increases the cost of its production. The total cost of renting a house is therefore increased by the poor rate, and consequently the poor rates fall partly on the occupier of a house. The owner of the land bears the incidence of that part of the poor rate which is calculated on the ground rent; the occupier bears the incidence of the rate levied on the value of the house.

The Incidence of Poor Rates levied on Trade premises. In the case of trade premises, manufactories, etc. the poor rates must also be divided into two portions; that levied on the land being borne by the owner of the land, and that levied on the buildings being borne by the consumers of the commodities which are manufactured in the buildings. Take, for example, the incidence of the poor rates levied on a cotton mill. Let it be assumed that they amount to £150 annually. The cost of producing a given quantity of cotton goods is thus increased by £150, and as it has been shown that the price of commodities which can be indefinitely increased is always ultimately regulated by cost of production, it is evident that the poor rate increases the price of cotton goods, or, in other words, the incidence of the rate is on the consumer. But it may be urged that the rate varies in different localities; that in one parish the rate levied on certain premises may be £100, and in another parish the rate levied on similar premises may be £300. If these premises are both used to produce the same commodities, what influence will these different rates have on the prices of the commodities? It is a principle of political economy that the price of a commodity is regulated by the cost of producing that portion whose cost of production is the highest.

The price of vessels is regulated by the cost of producing those vessels whose cost of production is the highest. If the price were less, the vessels built under the most disadvantageous circumstances would cease to yield the ordinary rate of profit to capital and the average rate of wages to labor. But it must be remembered that at the same time the manufacturers who are carrying on business under more favorable circumstances are realizing exceptionally large profits. There is therefore every inducement for them to increase the supply. If this increased supply takes place, or if there is a decrease in the demand, the equalization between supply and demand is effected by a lowering of the price. Under these circumstances the most heavily burdened part of the shipbuilding trade ceases to be profitable and gradually ceases to exist. This describes what actually took place in 1870 in the London shipbuilding trade. The poor rates and other charges were so enormously high in the east end of London, that when the exceptional demand for vessels caused by the American war fell off, and the price of vessels consequently declined, the shipbuilding trade of London was virtually destroyed: such vessels as were required being built on the Tyne and the Clyde. Every shipbuilding yard that was closed hastened the closing of the rest in the same locality; for by throwing hundreds of artisans out of employment pauperism was increased and the amount of the poor rate was necessarily augmented. The burdens on the depressed industry thus speedily accumulated, and gradually but surely the shipbuilding trade declined on the Thames. The incidence of poor rates in such a case as this is borne by the capitalists and laborers engaged in the depressed industry, and the poor rate may be perhaps in such an instance accused of causing more misery than it alleviates. It is a most serious national misfortune when the amount of the poor rate is so great as to maim or destroy a once prosperous branch of industry. No remedy for this paralyzing influence of the poor rate can be provided by the well-meant efforts of private charity. No permanent benefit will result from individual exertions or legislative enactments unless they tend to weaken the causes which produce pauperism.

QUESTIONS ON CHAPTER III. *ON TAXATION*

1. Why is taxation necessary?
2. Ought any class of persons who avail themselves of the protection which a state affords to enjoy immunity from taxation?
3. Enumerate Adam Smith's four canons of taxation.
4. In what manner only can the first canon be observed?
5. Why is the nonobservance of the second canon detrimental to trade?
6. Illustrate the importance of the third canon.
7. Point out the connection between the third and the fourth canon.
8. Describe the utility of bonding houses.
9. What is the effect of the use of the bonding house on the price of the commodities lodged therein?
10. In accordance with the fourth canon, ought taxes to be levied on raw material or on manufactured commodities?
11. Why does a tax on raw material increase the price of the manufactured commodity by an amount far exceeding the revenue yielded to the state?
12. Why would direct taxation on commodities sold in shops be impractical?
13. Which is the most obvious way of carrying out the fourth canon?
14. What is the difference between direct and indirect taxation?
15. What is meant by the incidence of taxation?
16. What is the income tax?
17. Ought temporary and permanent incomes to be taxed at the same rate?
18. Give illustrations showing that temporary and permanent incomes ought to be taxed at the same rate if the income tax is fixed in amount and permanent.
19. Why would it be impractical to adjust the income tax according to the capitalized value of each income?
20. Why does the income tax press more severely on the possessor of a small income than on the possessor of a large income?
21. What remedy has been suggested for this inequality?

22. What modification of this plan has been adopted?

23. Is the income tax invariably a direct tax?

24. When income tax is paid out of capital, on whom does the tax chiefly fall?

25. Is the opportunity of evading the payment of the full amount of income tax, which some people avail themselves of, a valid objection to the tax?

26. It has been laid down as an axiom, that each ought to contribute to the imperial exchequer a certain fixed proportion of his superfluities. What effect would this rule have in deciding what commodities should be taxed?

27. Who bears the incidence of all taxes levied on land?

28. What is the land tax?

29. Describe its magnitude in England and in India.

30. What important principle is recognized by the existence of a land tax?

31. Explain the economic perfection of a land tenure in which all rents are paid to the State.

32. What would be the consequence of the land tax exceeding the economic rent?

33. What are tithes, what was their original purpose, and by whom are they now frequently owned?

34. What are the main provisions of the Tithe Commutation Act?

35. What effect has this Act had on the amount of the tithes?

36. Who bears the incidence of poor rates in the case of house property?

37. Prove that the occupier of the house bears part of the incidence of the poor rate.

38. Who bears the incidence of the poor rate levied on trade premises?

39. What is the effect of an excessive poor rate in depressing industry?

40. Describe the decline of the shipbuilding trade on the Thames.

41. When the burden of the poor rate is such as to destroy a branch of industry, on whom does the real burden fall?

    (*a*) It was said that tax payers were never asked by the collector whether they approved of this or that application of public money; but do not the tax payers then control the national expenditure? Have they not a right to do so? How far does the parliamentary suffrage confer this power on the taxpayers?

(b) Were the taxes on hair powder and on windows direct or indirect?

(c) If all the land in England belonged to the nation, so that all farmers paid their rent to the Government, would taxation be increased or diminished?

Endnotes

SECTION I
CHAPTER I

[1] The French socialist Fourier, in the scheme which he elaborated for the reconstruction of society, placed "Talent" among the requisites of Production, and assigned to it a certain definite share (one-fourth) of the wealth resulting from the combined efforts of the members of the society.

SECTION II
CHAPTER III

[1] The population of England and Wales increased between the years 1841 and 1871 from 15,914,148 to 22,712,266.

CHAPTER IV

[1] It might appear from the foregoing paragraph that in order to settle the account between England and India it would be necessary for England in 1876 to have transmitted £16,000,000 in cash to India. For some years however this debt which England owes to India for "goods delivered" has been canceled and more than canceled by the debt which India owes to England for interest on debt, cost of transport and recruiting soldiers, payment of salaries and pensions, etc. These "Home charges" which India owes to England amount annually to about £17,000,000, so that when the balance is finally struck, it is India which is in debt to England and not vice versa.

SECTION III
CHAPTER I

[1] Productiveness is here and in other places intended to signify both fertility and convenience of situation.

CHAPTER IV

[1] To give an idea of the importance of some of these societies it may be stated that in 1876 the Amalgamated Carpenters and Joiners' Union had 317 branches, 16,038 members, and a cash balance in hand of £70,109. The Amalgamated Engineers' had 44,578 members, an income of more than £100,000 a year, and a cash balance of £275,146. The Ironfounders had 12,336 members, and an income of £31,000 a year. These figures are taken from the accounts published in *The Conflicts of Capital and Labor* by Mr. George Howell.

[2] I am indebted to Mr. W. H. Hall for kindly furnishing me with the details of M. Leclaire's scheme of cooperation.

SECTION IV
CHAPTER I

[1] Many paragraphs of this petition have been omitted; but it is hoped that nothing has been left out which is essential to the line of argument adopted.

CHAPTER III

[1] It has been objected to this statement that the State loses by this transaction all that the consumer gains; that if the duly had been paid directly the wine was imported, the State would have had the £500 six months sooner, and could thus have gained the six months' interest on that sum. But this argument assumes that the State can lay out its money at as high an interest as the private merchant. We have estimated the wine merchant's annual profits to be 20 percent. The State could not probably obtain more than 3 percent. Half a year's interest on £500 at 3 percent per annum is £7. 10s. Therefore, though the State might gain this amount if the duty had been paid six months earlier, the consumer would in consequence have to pay the £50 extra for his wine, out of which sum the State would only benefit to the extent of £7. 10s. £42. 10s. would have to be paid in consequence of the tax more than ever reaches in any shape the revenue of the State.

INDEX

Printed in the United States
by Baker & Taylor Publisher Services